TOTALLY OBSESSED

A Journal for the

AWESOME, RANDOM,

AND WEIRD STUFF

YOU LOVE

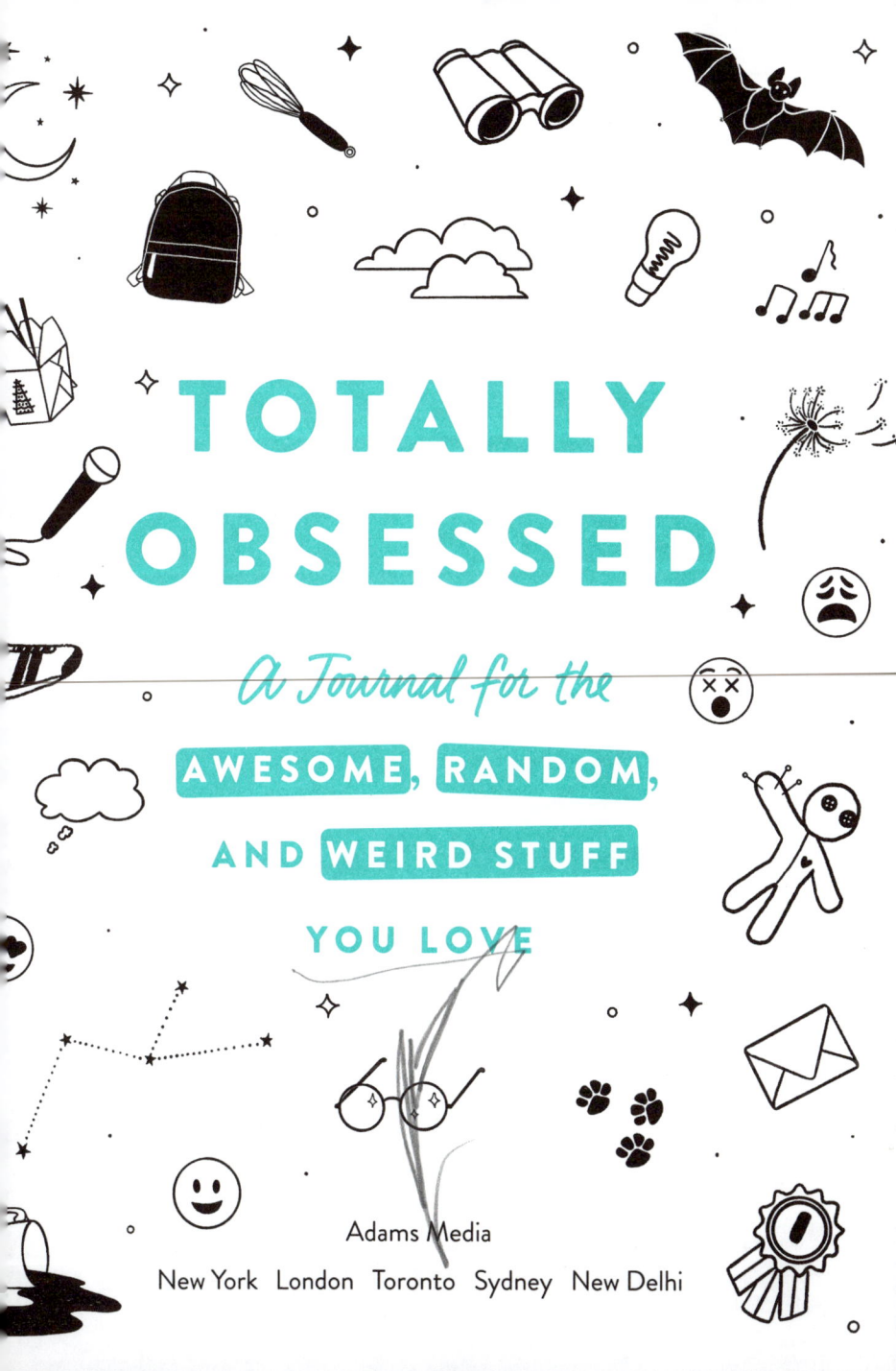

TOTALLY OBSESSED

A Journal for the

AWESOME, RANDOM, AND WEIRD STUFF

YOU LOVE

Adams Media

New York London Toronto Sydney New Delhi

Adams Media
An Imprint of Simon & Schuster, Inc.
100 Technology Center Drive
Stoughton, Massachusetts 02072

First Adams Media hardcover edition December 2021

ADAMS MEDIA and colophon are trademarks of Simon & Schuster.

For information about special discounts for bulk purchases, please contact Simon & Schuster Special Sales at 1-866-506-1949 or business@simonandschuster.com.

The Simon & Schuster Speakers Bureau can bring authors to your live event. For more information or to book an event contact the Simon & Schuster Speakers Bureau at 1-866-248-3049 or visit our website at www.simonspeakers.com.

Interior design by Erin Alexander
Illustrations by Emma Taylor

Manufactured in the United States of America

1 2021

ISBN 978-1-5072-1790-0

THIS BOOK BELONGS TO:

Aubrey Ceballos
2022

INTRODUCTION

You have excellent taste—you *know* it. The things you love are awesome, and this journal is the perfect way to record and celebrate all of your favorite things. In these pages, you can gush about anything you want—hobbies you lose yourself in, the people and pets you love, songs you can't get out of your head, styles that make you swoon, characters and plotlines in your favorite series, the latest social media trends. You know, the stuff that makes you feel totally obsessed!

Inside, you'll find eighty-five fun, open-ended prompts to spark your creativity and help you capture all the wonderful, weird, or just random things living rent-free in your head. List *all* the things you low-key love. Record the things you can never have too much of! Or get as creative as you want and imagine a perfect world of your creation. Some pages have lines on which you can write your thoughts. Other pages have illustrations where you can write your responses. You can also get visual and draw your thoughts or create a collage using cut-out pictures and words. This is *your* journal. How you fill the pages is up to you!

Complete the pages in any order you wish. Choose the prompt that inspires you most in the moment. Have a friend who shares your obsession? Work on a prompt together. Return to a prompt any time you want to add a new idea or obsession. You never know when something new is going to capture your attention and rule your thoughts!

So whether you're keeping track of what makes you totally extra, describing your favorite place, or collecting everything you find cute and cuddly, just grab a pen, marker, or colored pencil, and get ready to pay tribute to the best things in *your* life in your own unique way. Hold nothing back. These are things you love to love! After all, there's absolutely nothing wrong with being 100% totally obsessed!

MOOD.

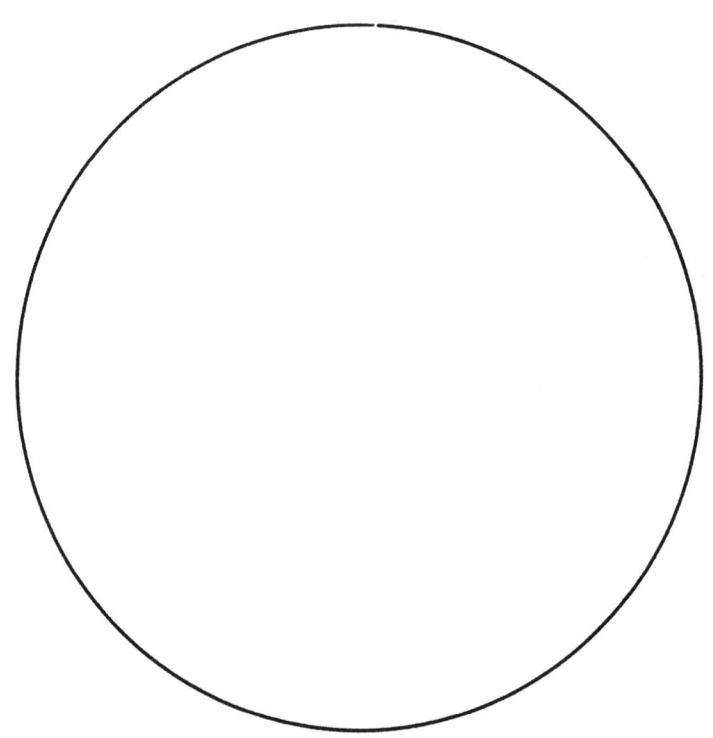

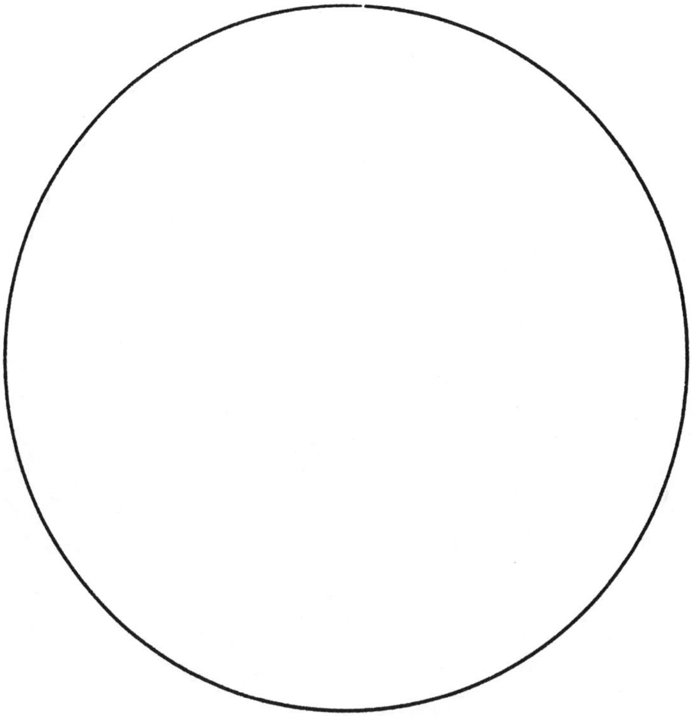

BUSY THINKING ABOUT...

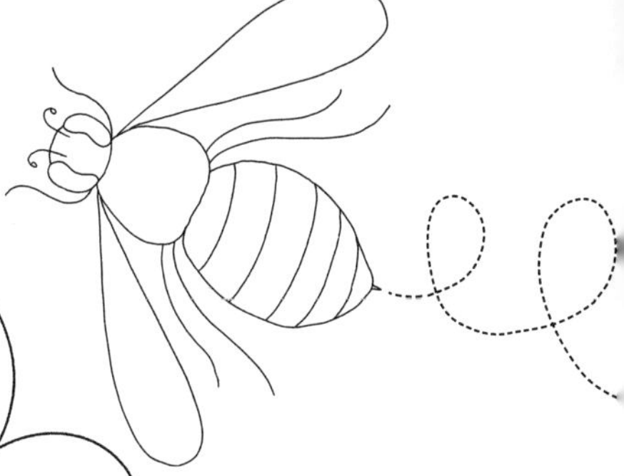

WHAT'S IN MY BAG?

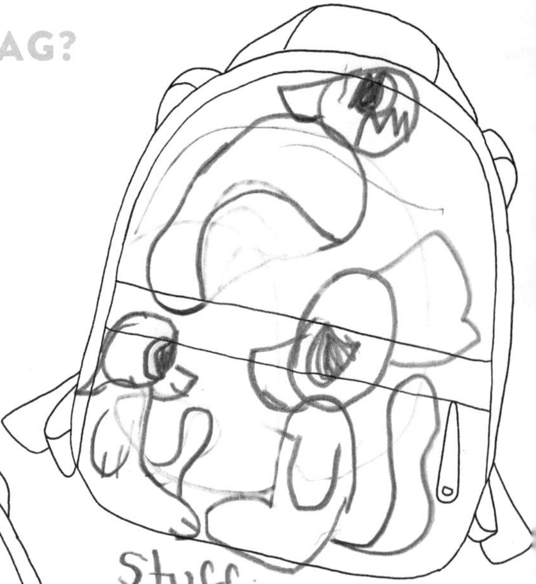

Stuffies

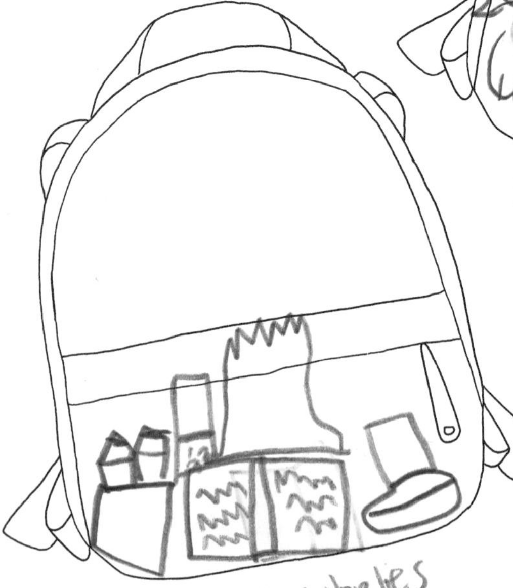

school supplies

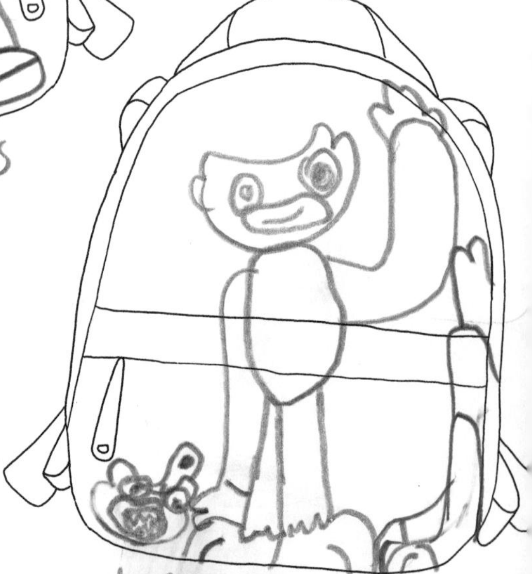

huggy wuggy

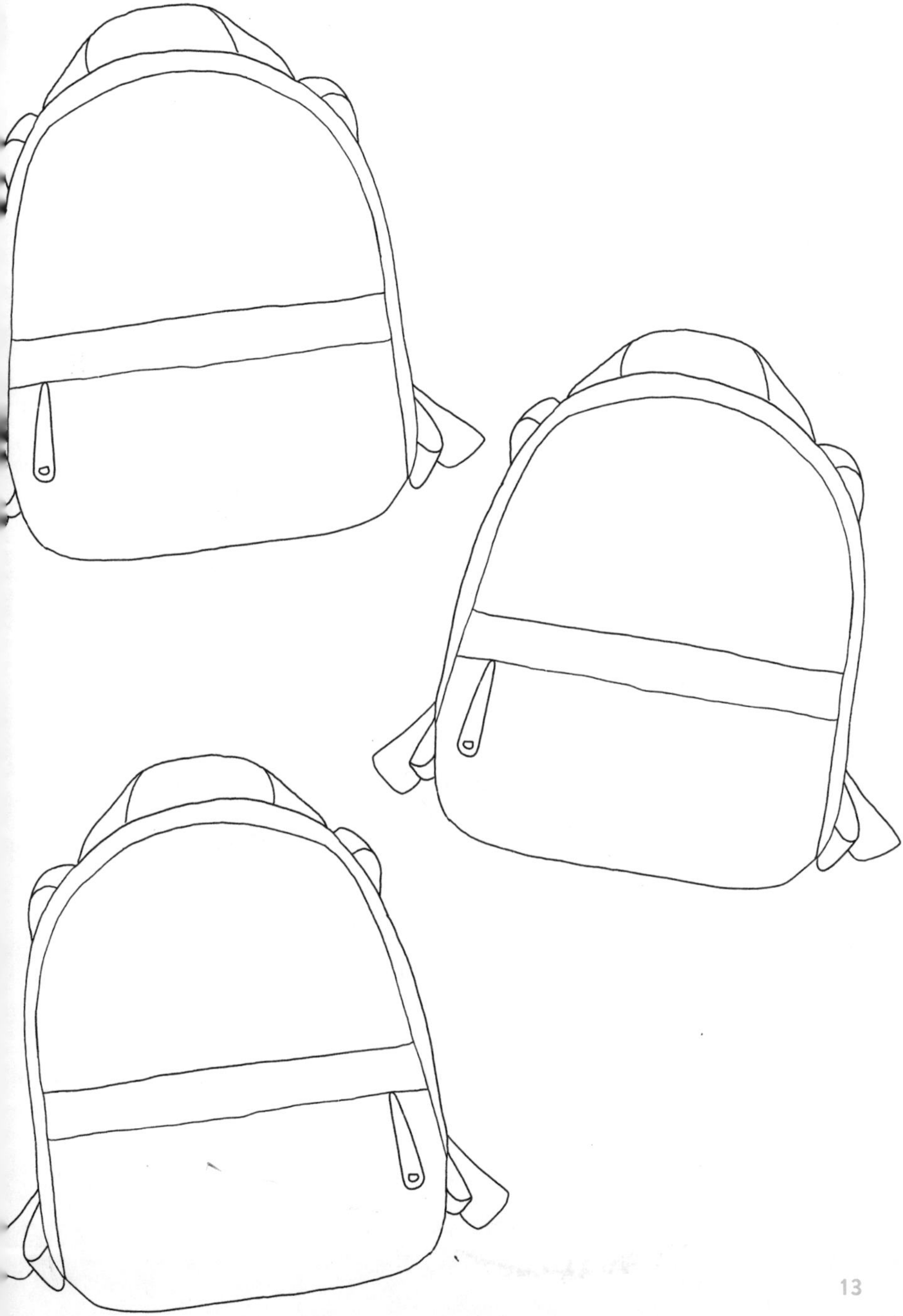

I NEED A SEQUEL TO...

_____

_____

_____

_____

_____

_____

_____

_____

The Story
Continues...

YOU CAN NEVER HAVE TOO MANY...

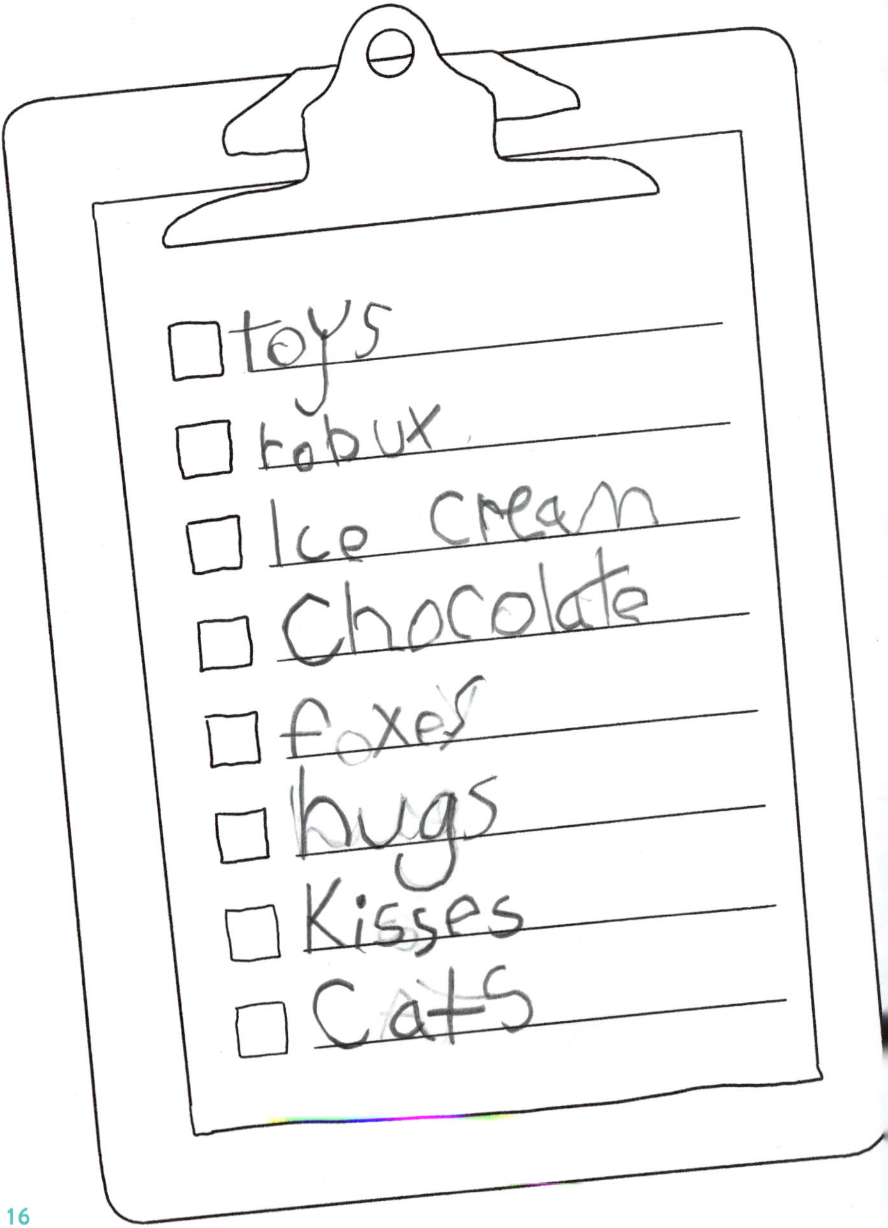
toys
robux
Ice cream
Chocolate
foxes
hugs
Kisses
Cats

4/4/2022

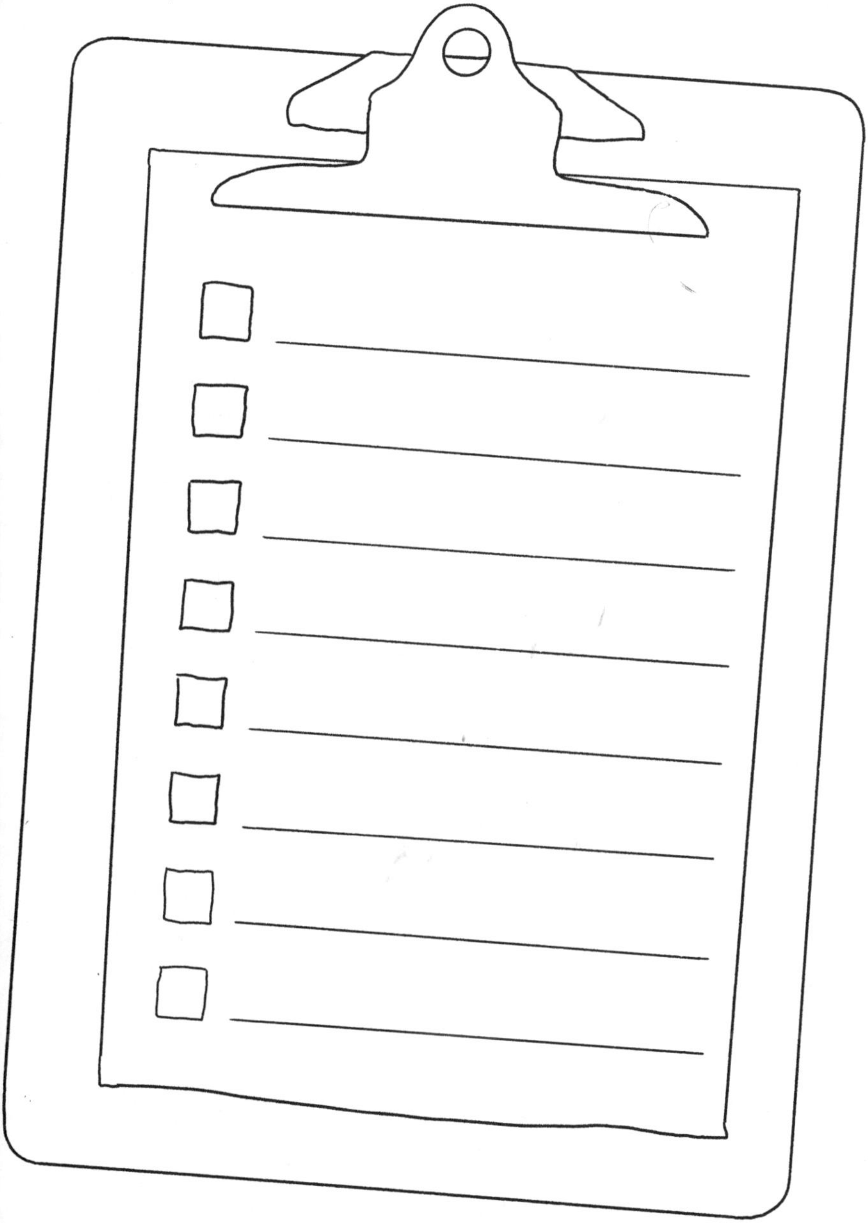

I WISH...

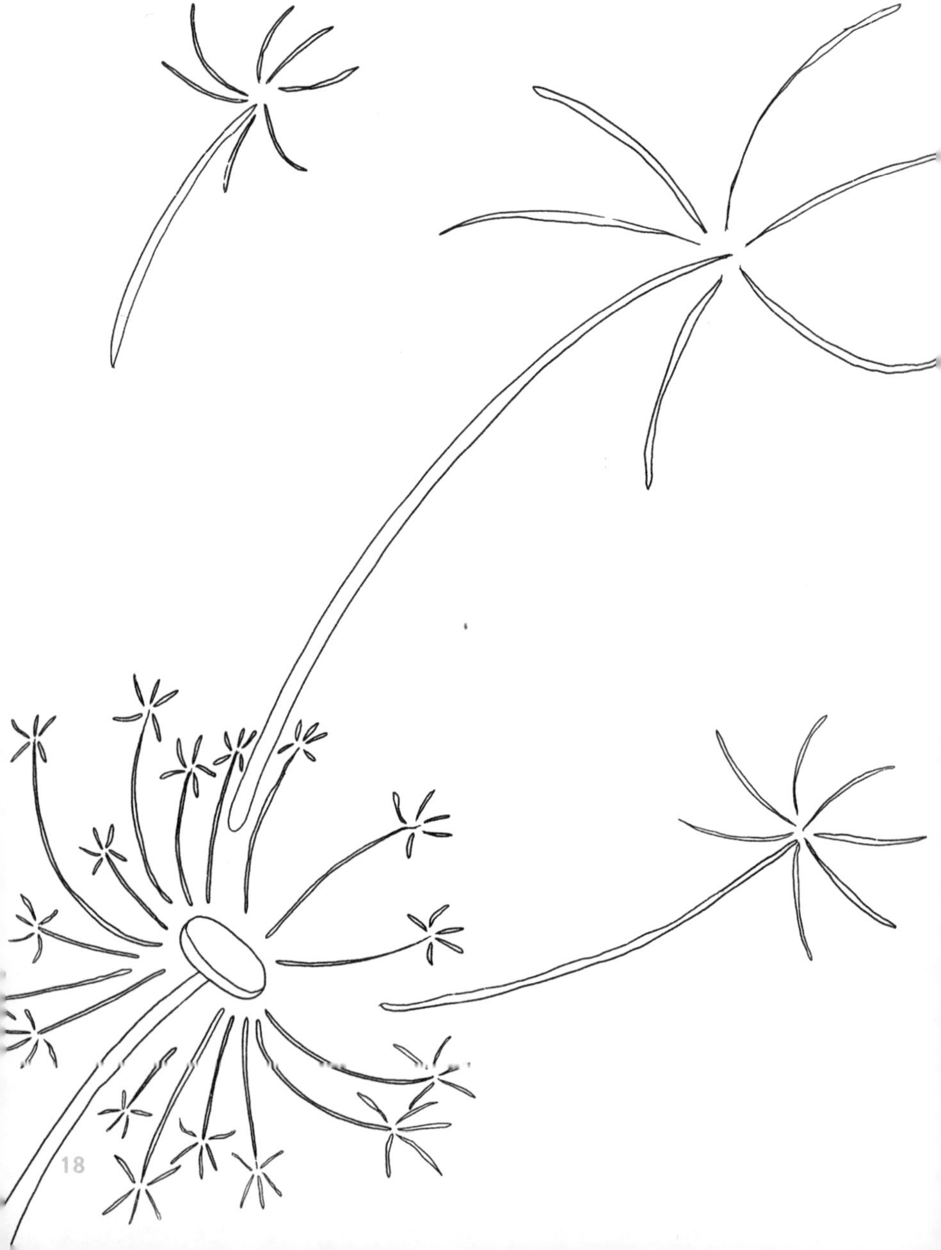

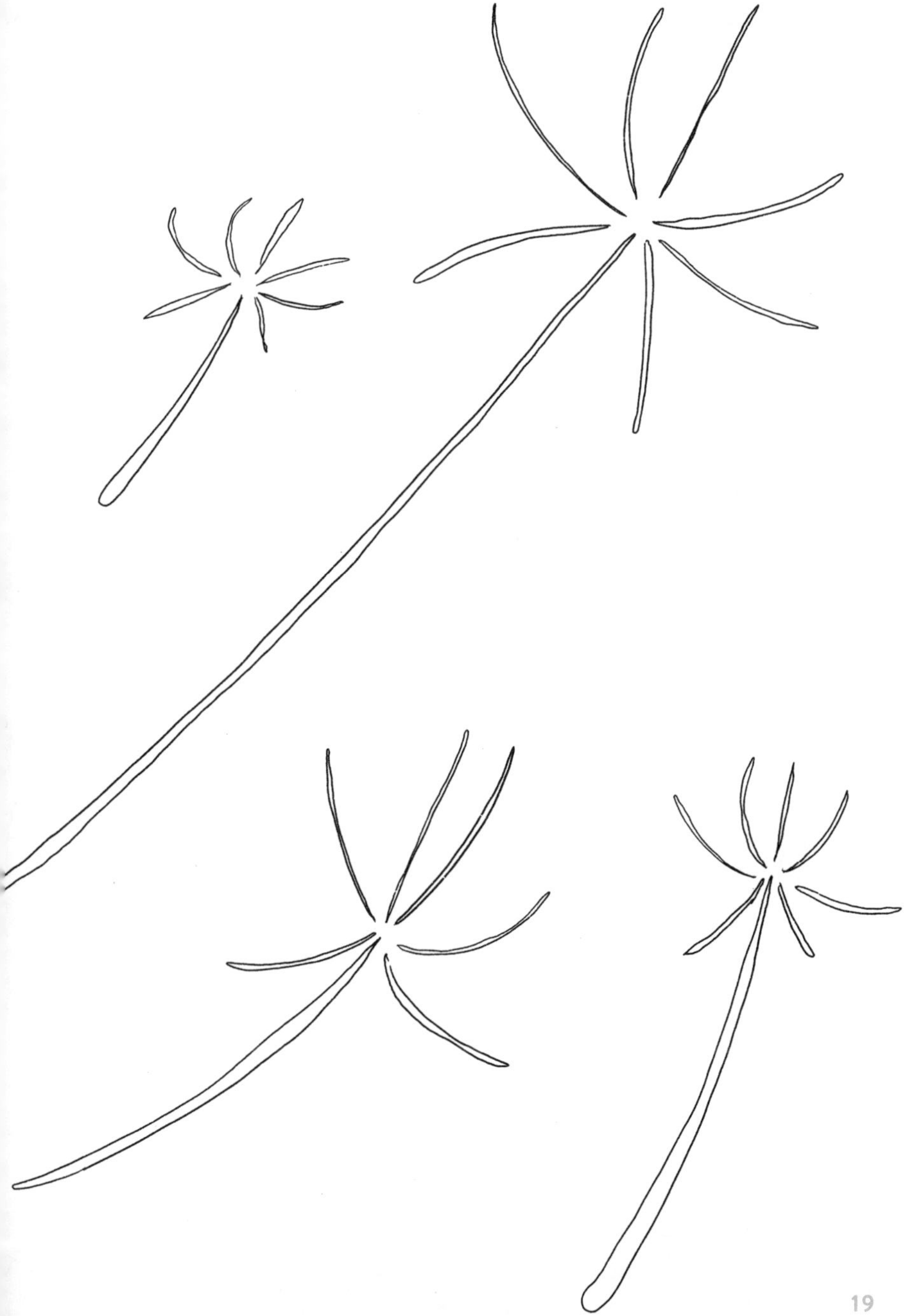

toys

hugs

Kiss

my bed

tanooki

Emily, Mom + Dad

Daya + Pa

warm + fluffy stuff

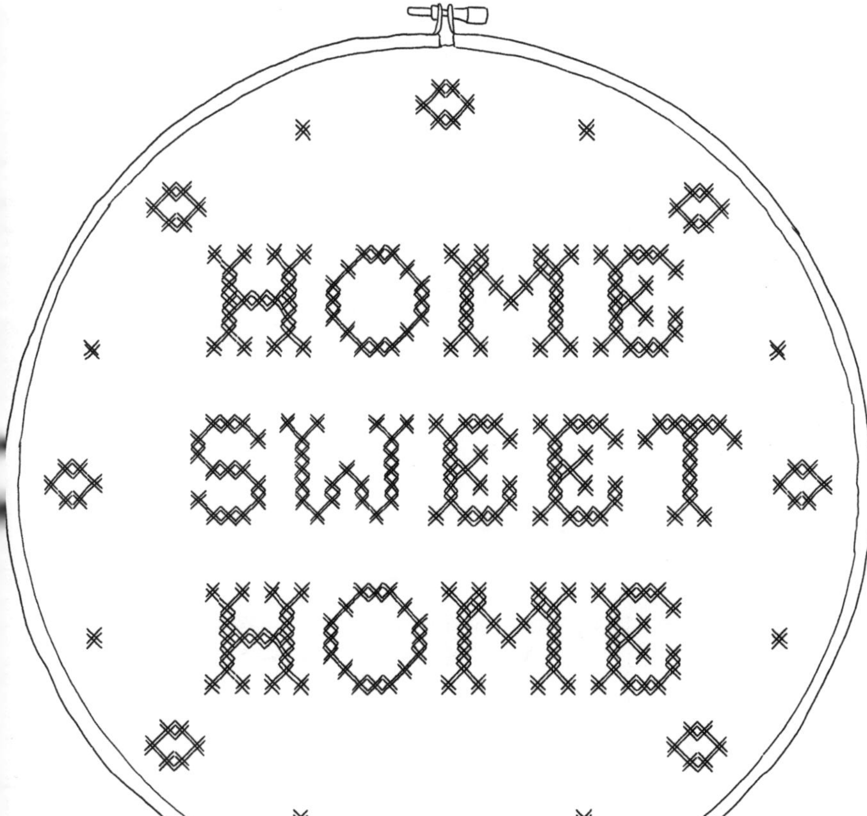
HOME
SWEET
HOME

FAN FIC

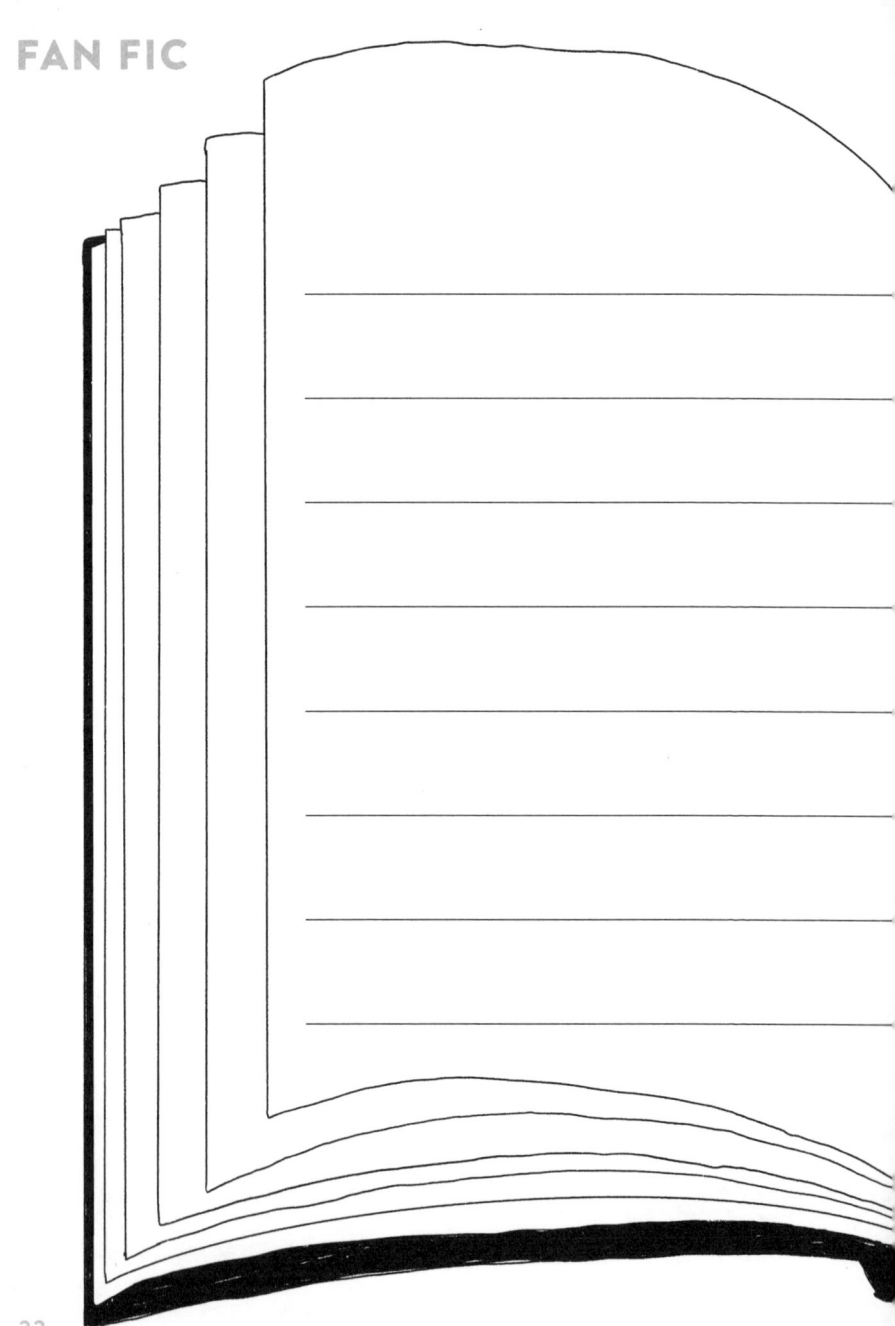

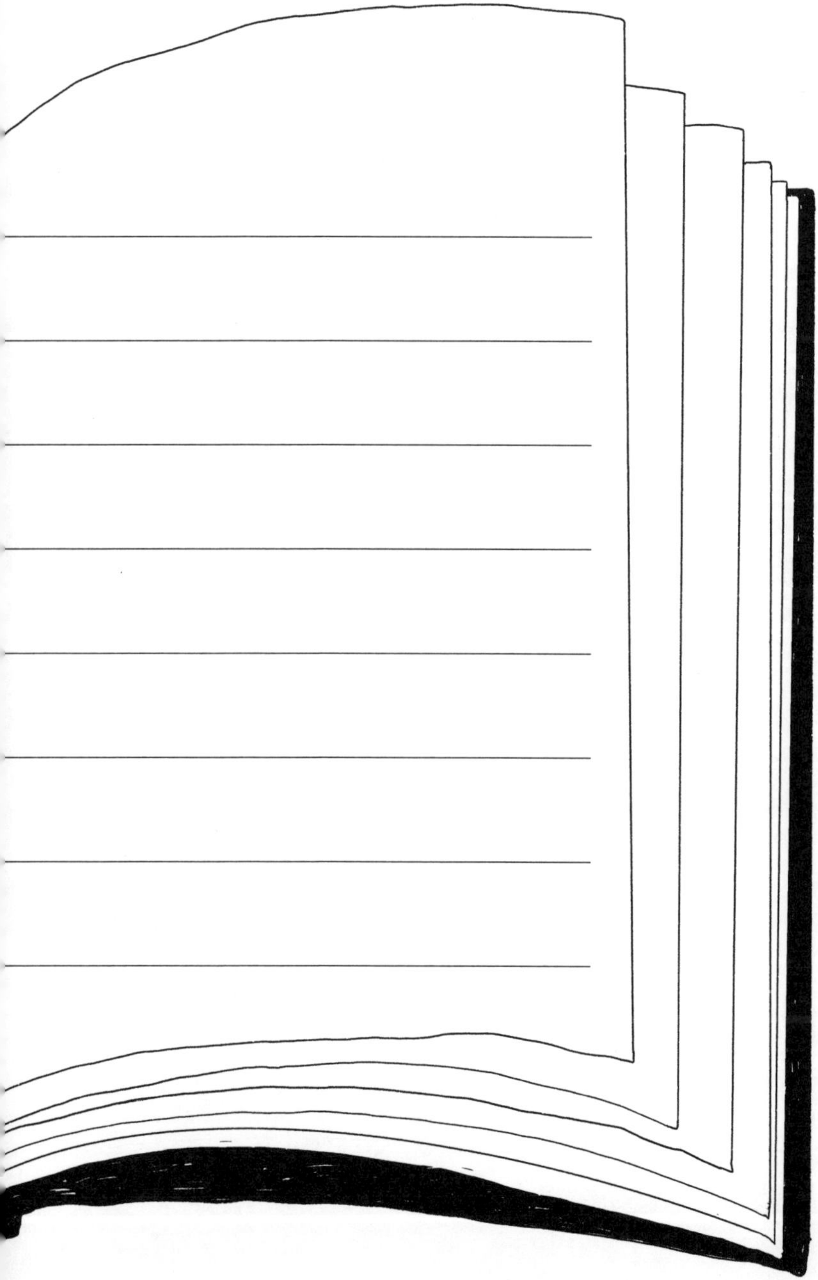

GOOD IDEAS

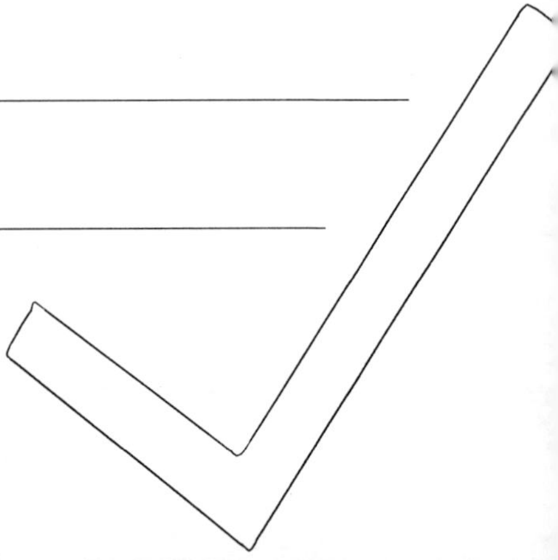

BAD IDEAS

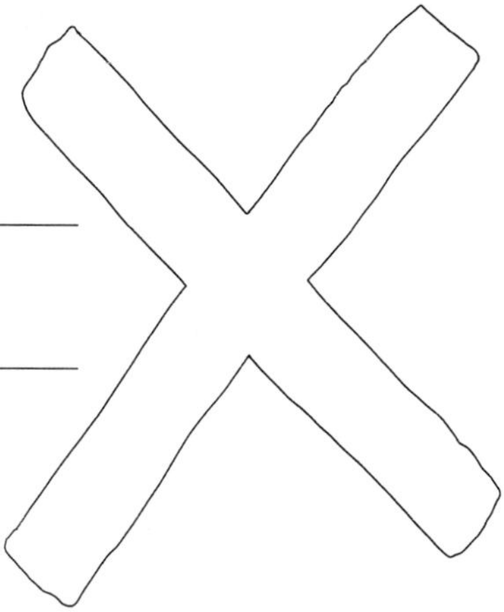

NOW PLAYING...

_____

_____

_____

_____

_____

_____

_____

MY FAVORITE PLACE

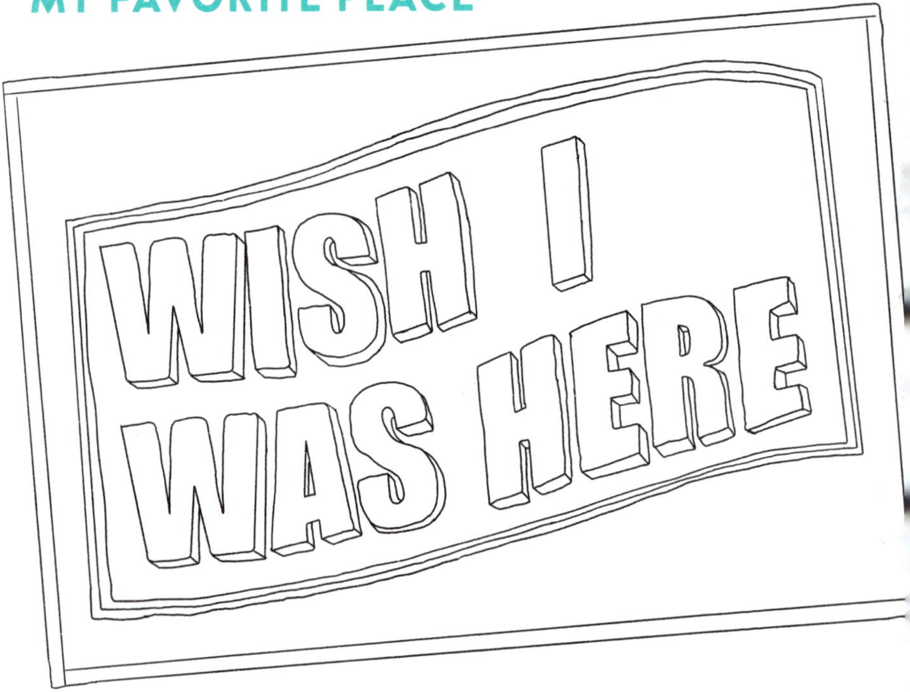
WISH I
WAS HERE

Home and the two playplaces my parents took me to. I like Daya's house because

It doesn't have scary
fire alarms and that
makes me happy in this
home.

MY SECRET RECIPE

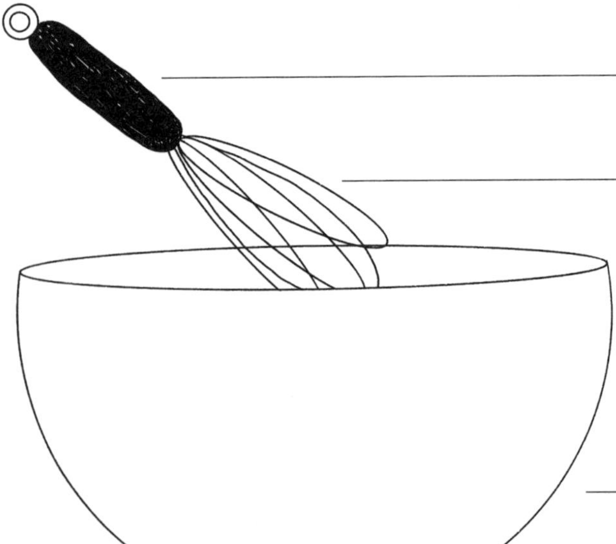

IS IT JUST ME, OR...

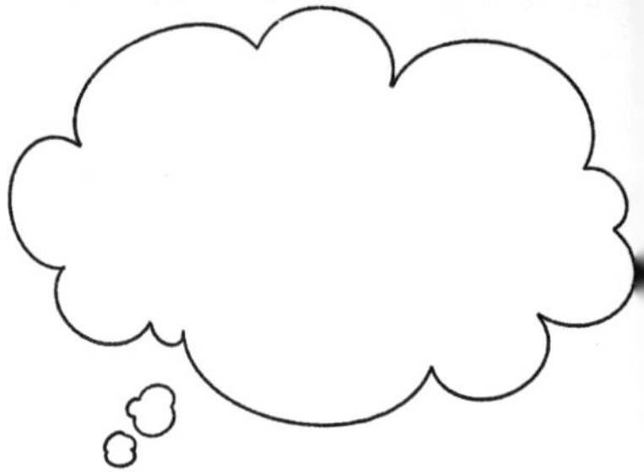

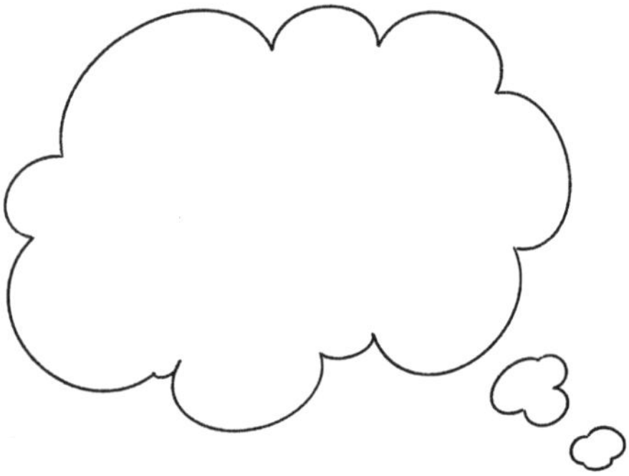

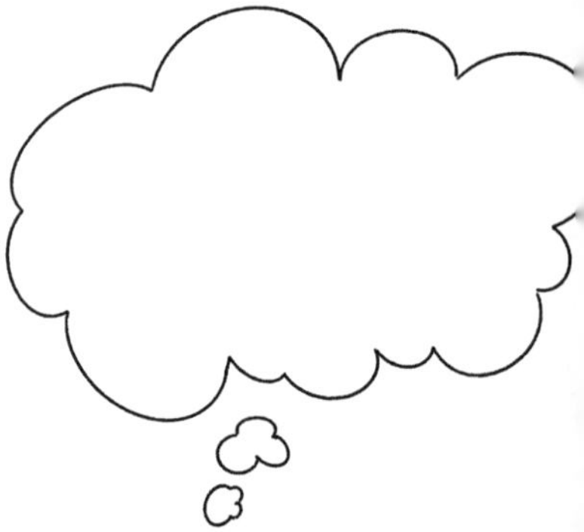

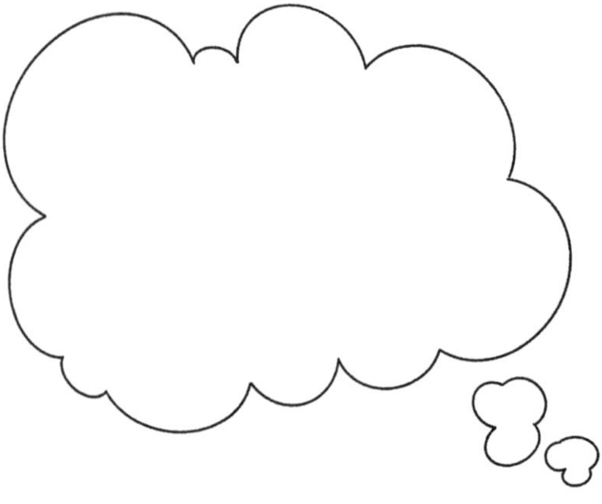

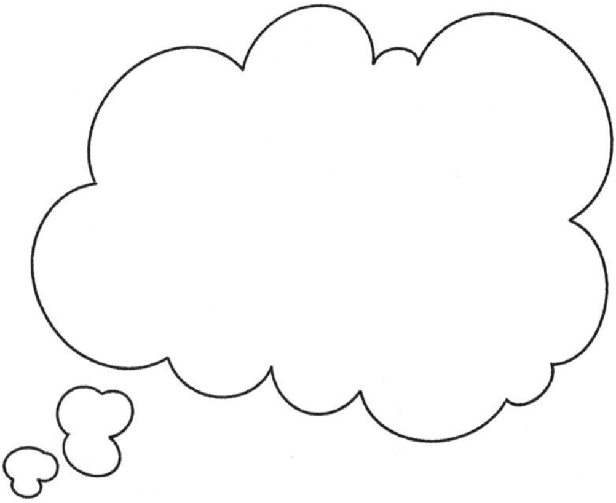

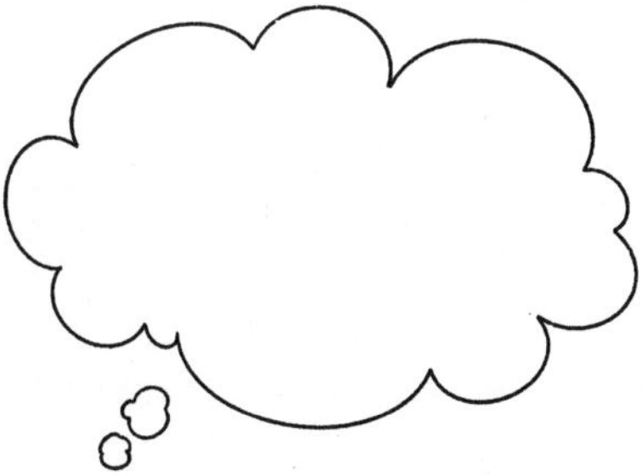

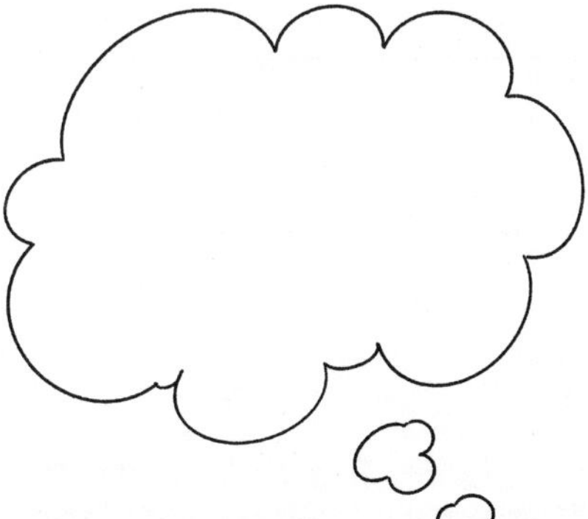

IN MY SEARCH HISTORY...

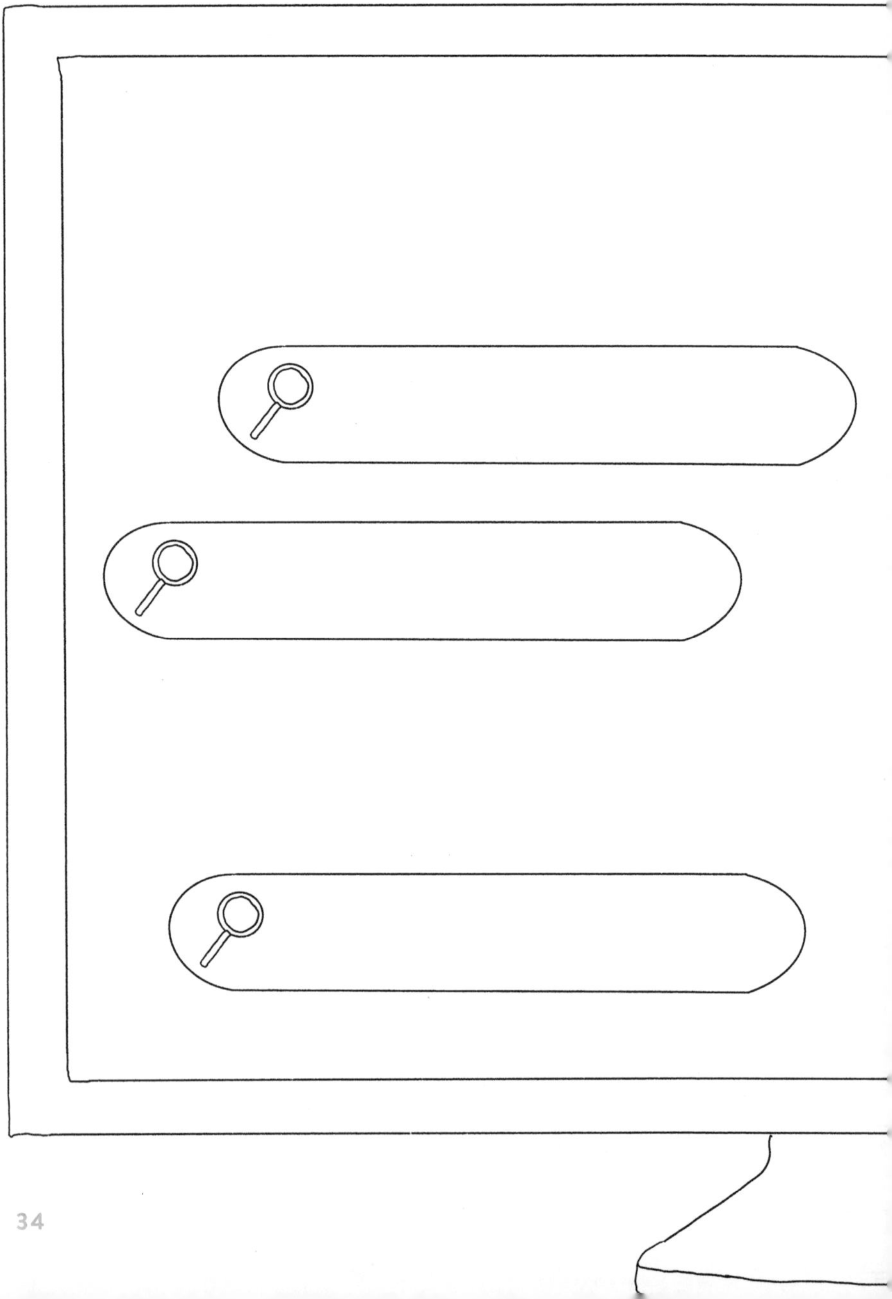

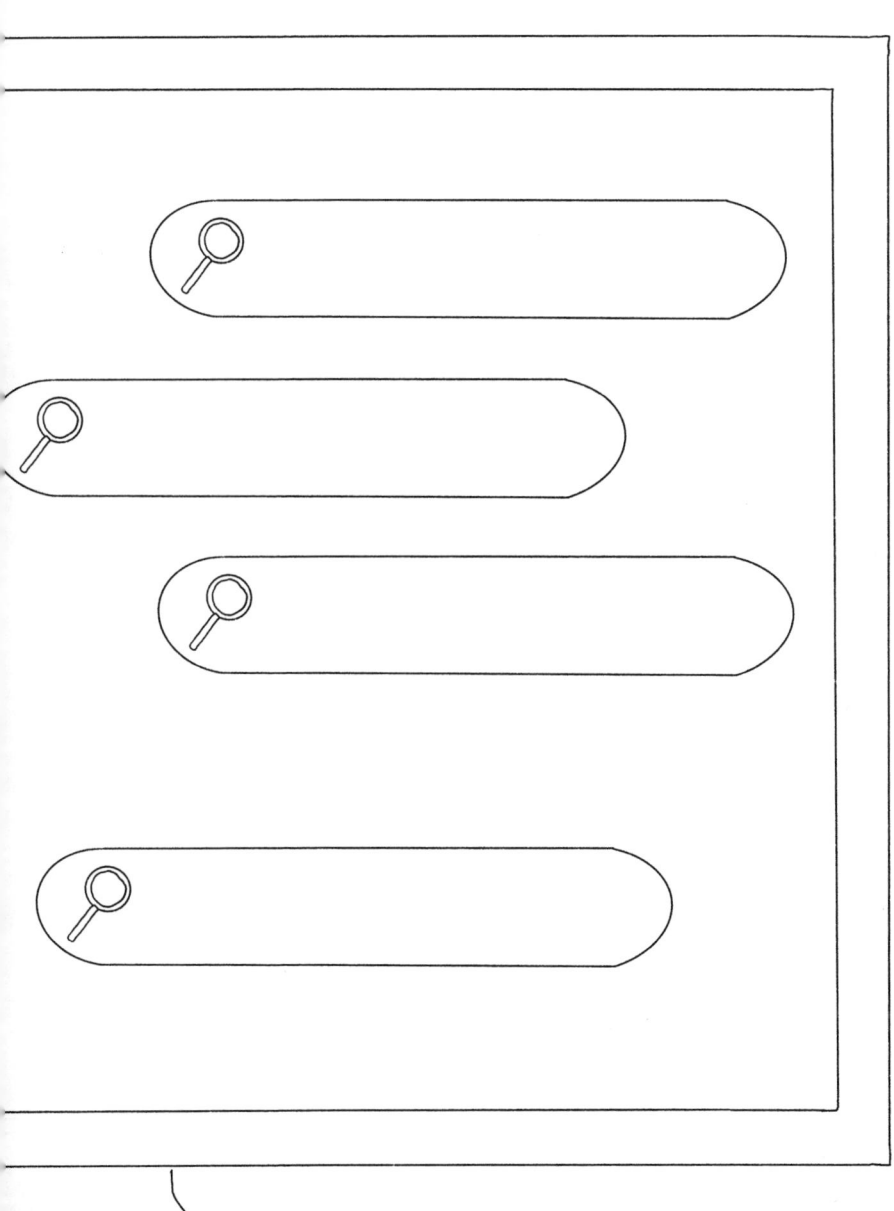

RUNNING ON REPEAT

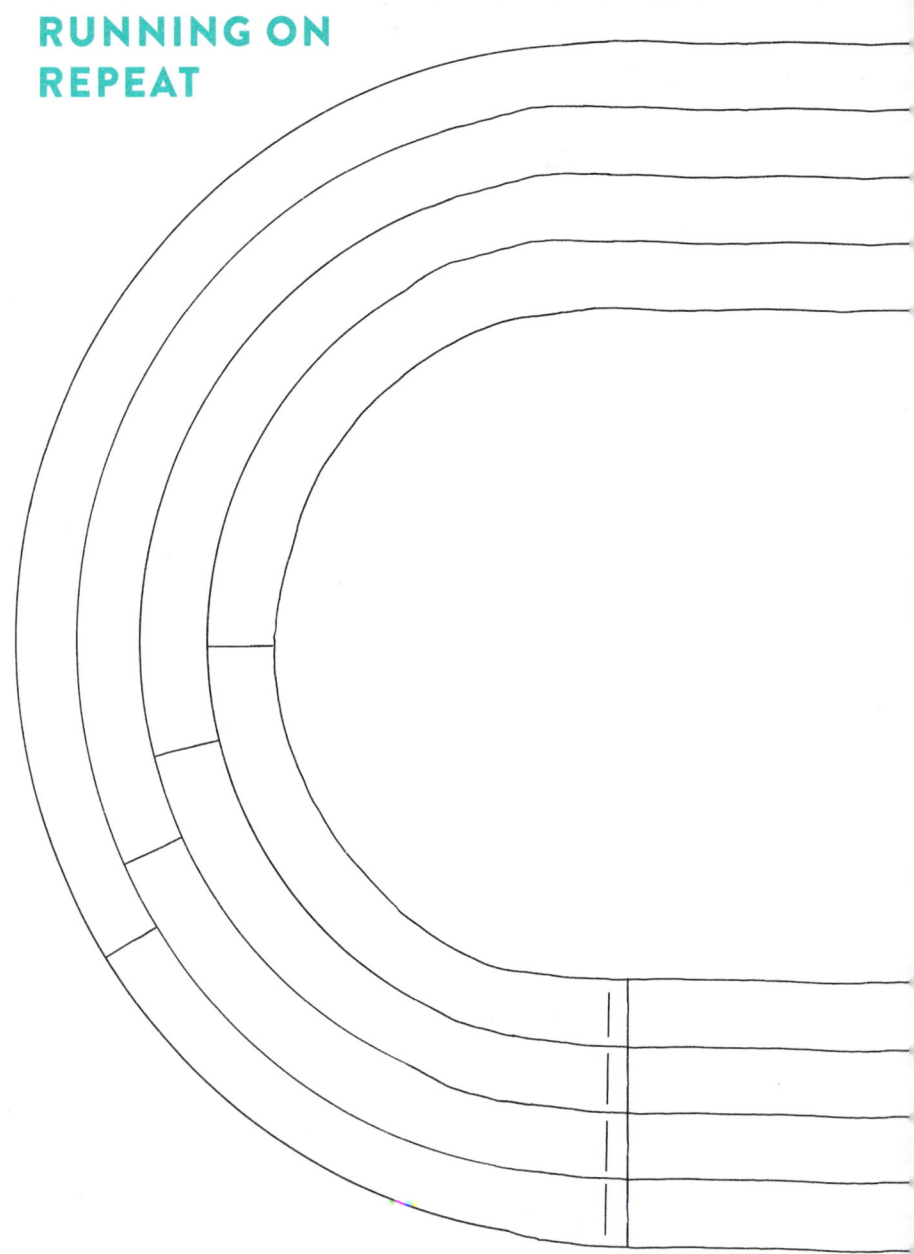

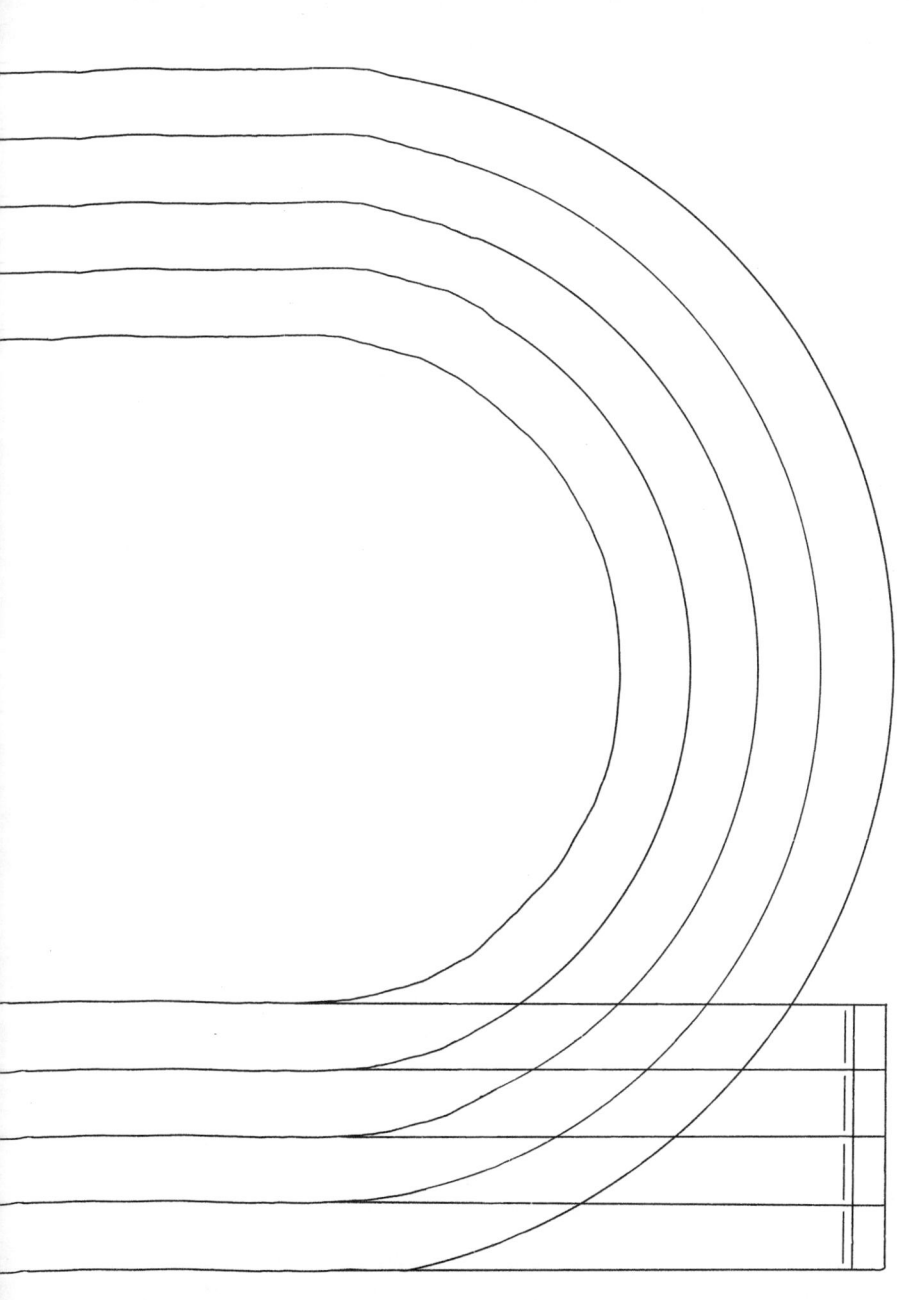

THINGS I HATE THAT EVERYONE ELSE LOVES

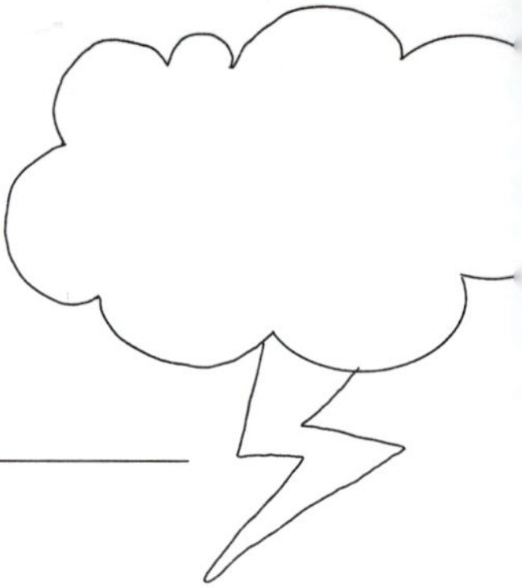

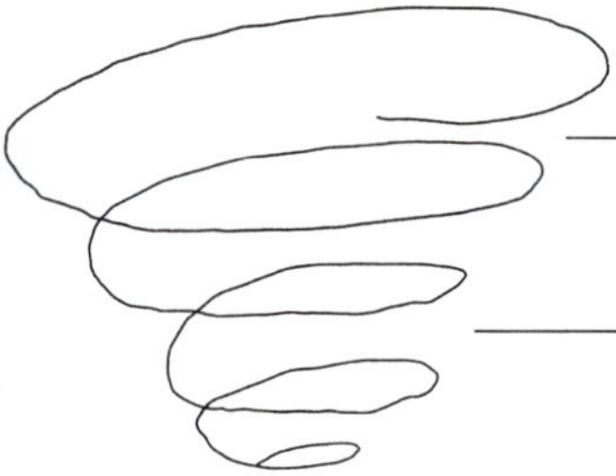

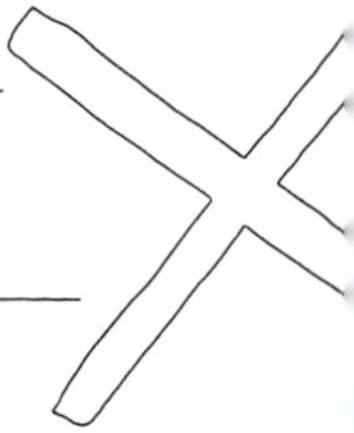

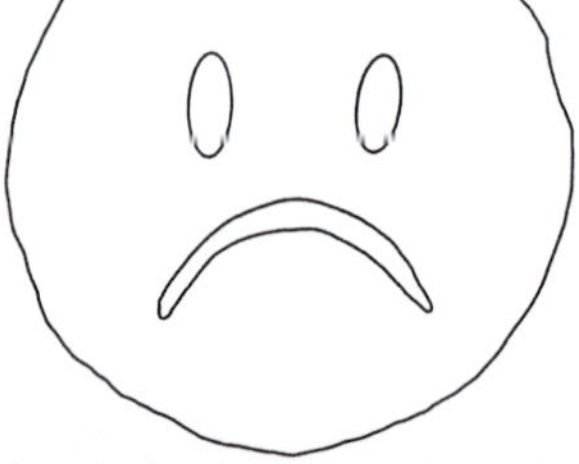

THINGS I LOVE THAT EVERYONE ELSE HATES

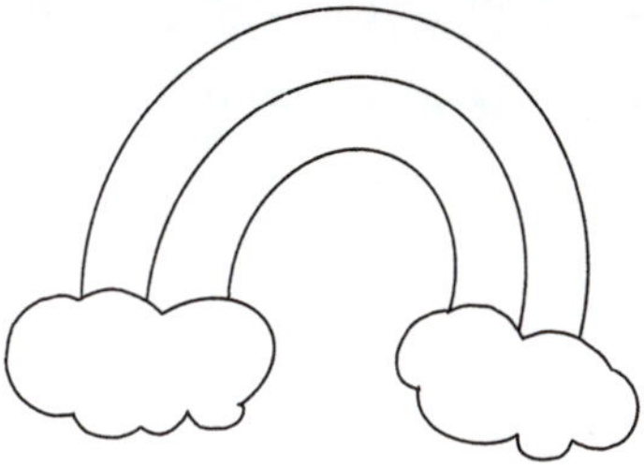

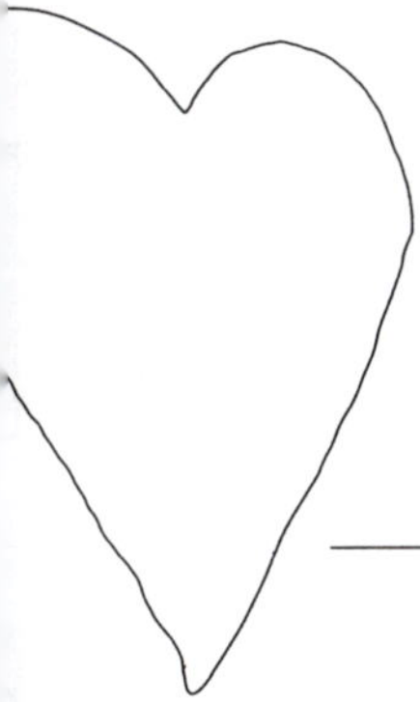

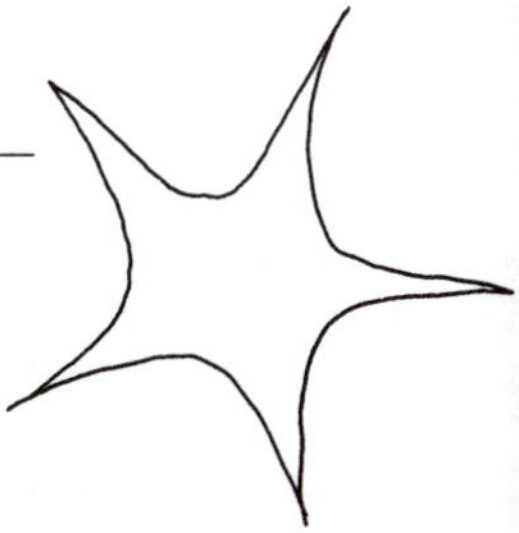

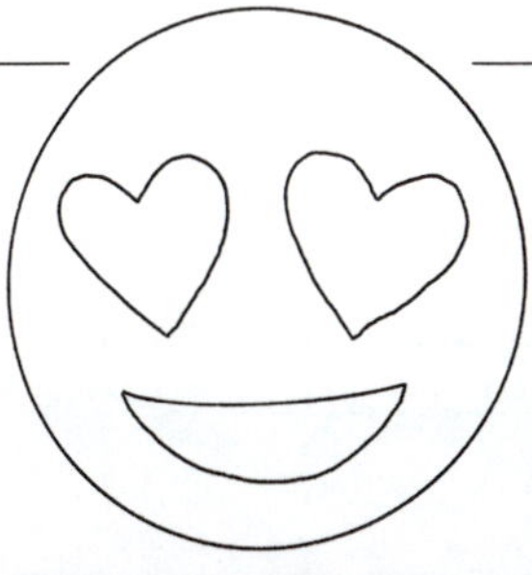

IN MY FEED...

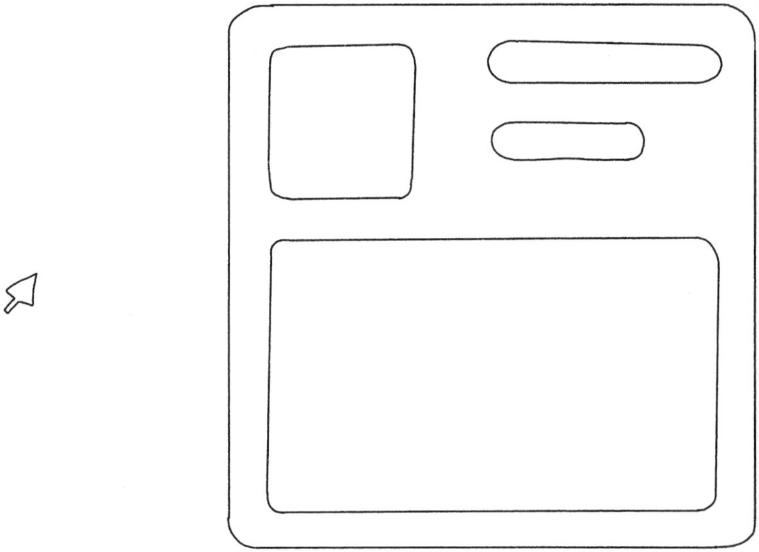

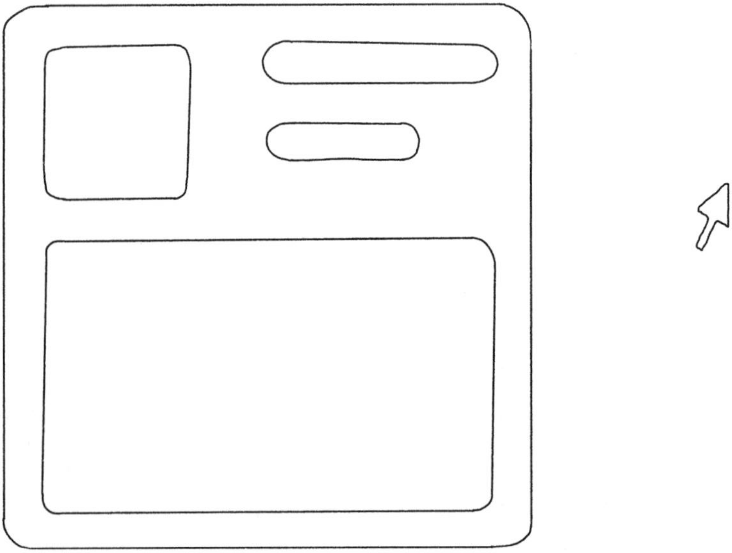

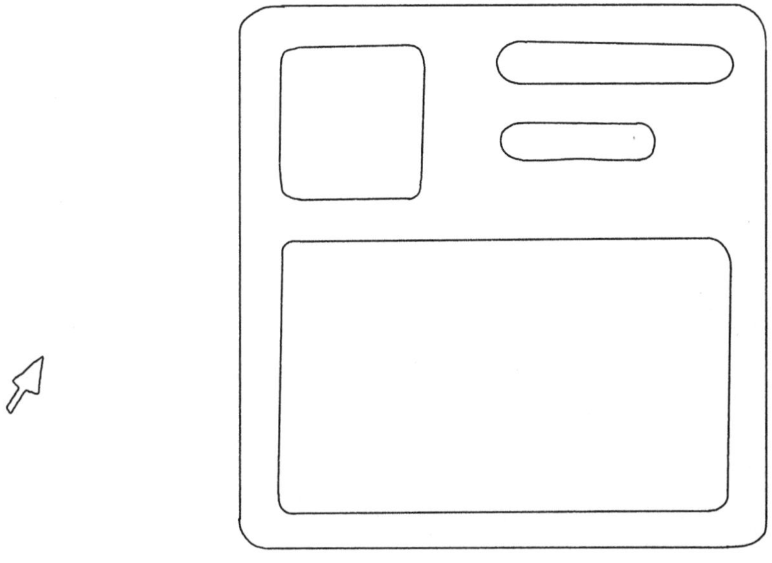

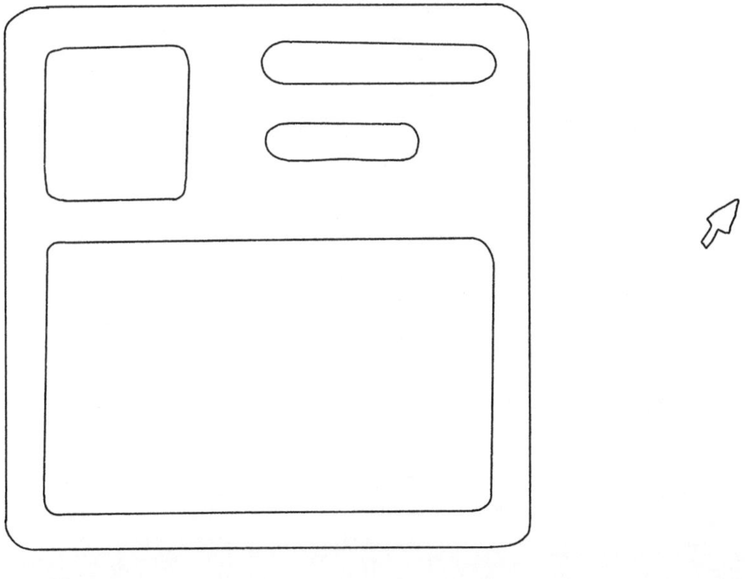

THINGS I WISH EVERYONE UNDERSTOOD...

¯_(ツ)_/¯

I KNOW WAY TOO MUCH ABOUT...

ACTUALLY KINDA TOXIC

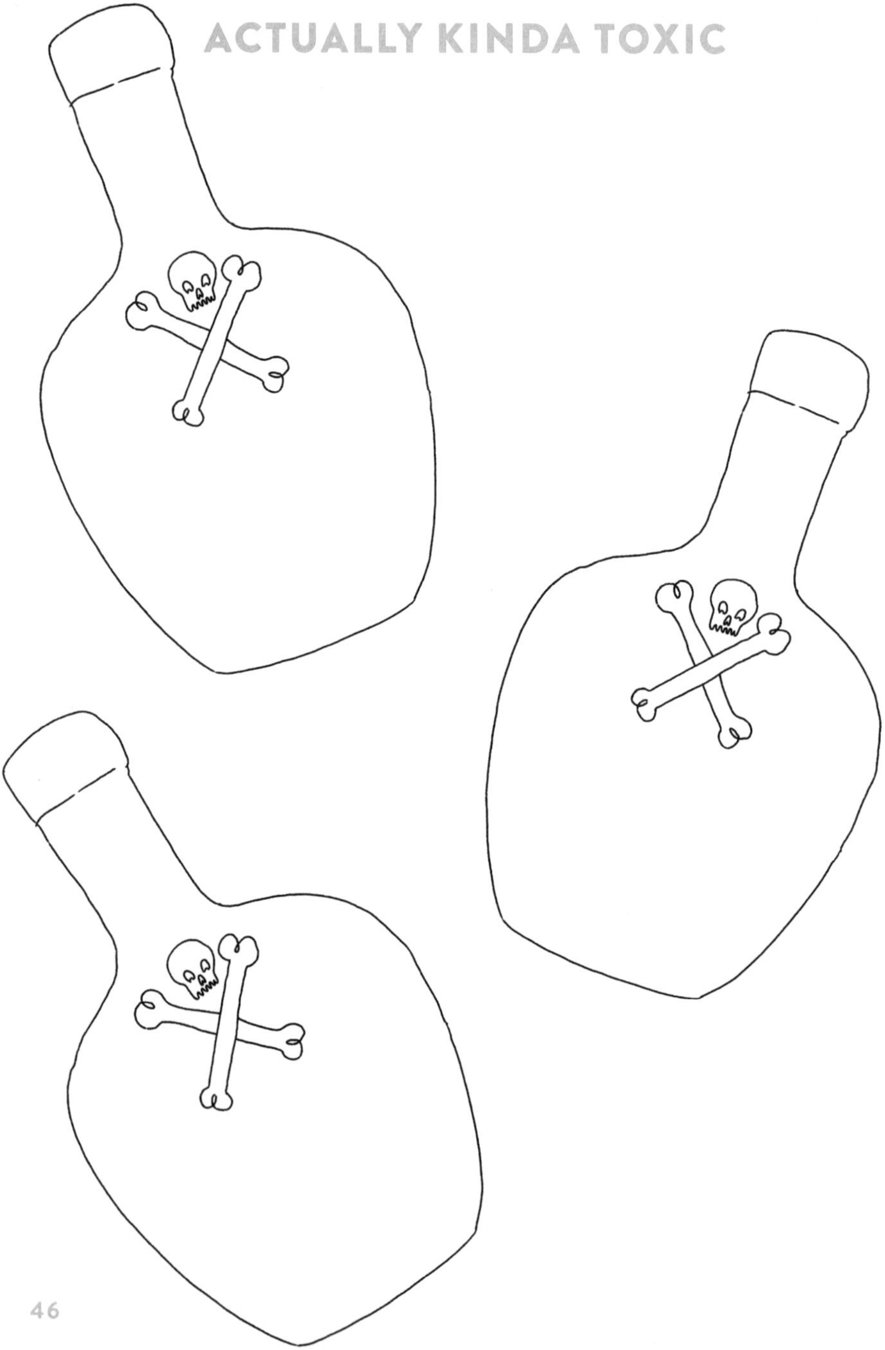

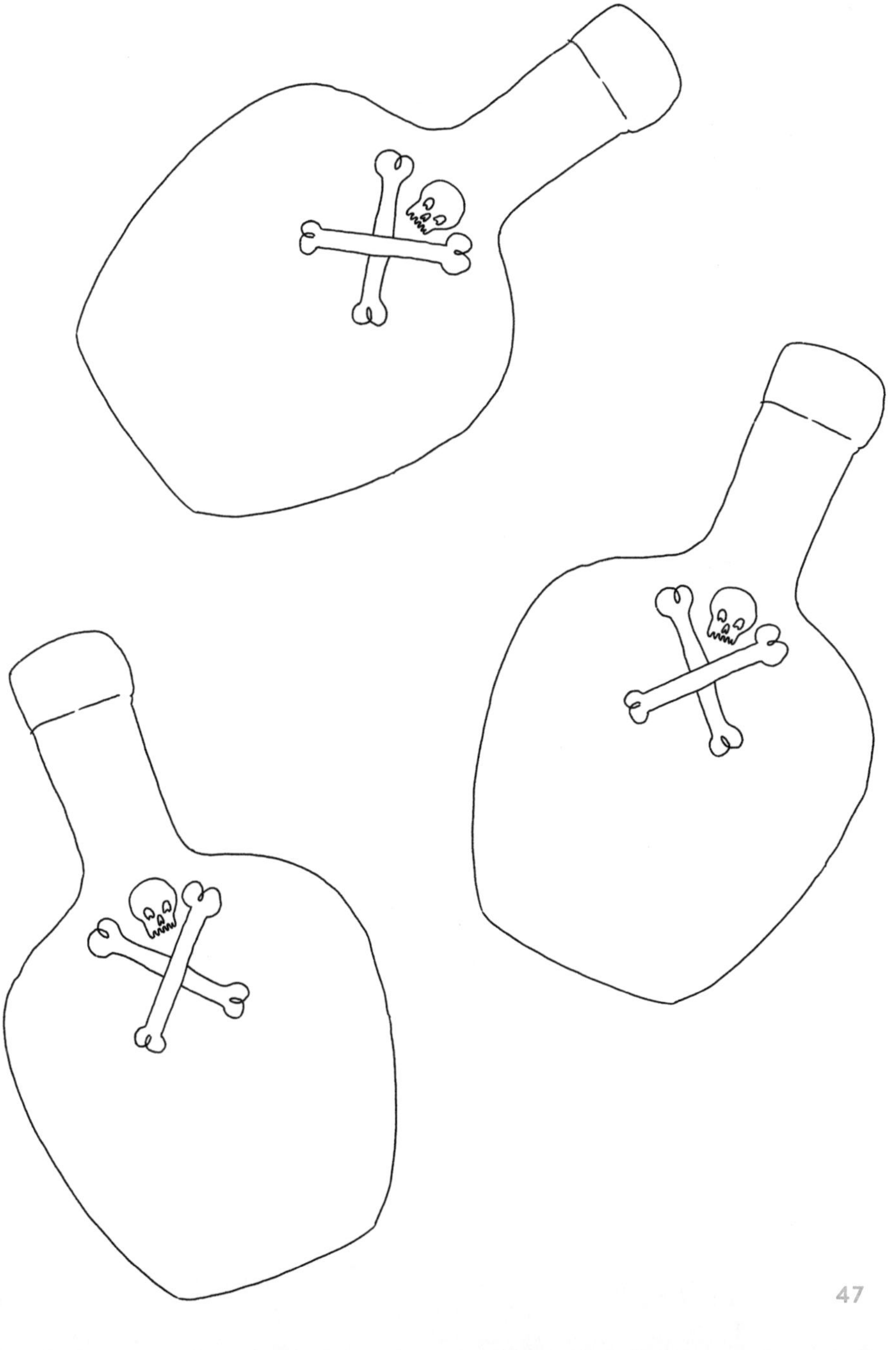

SPLURGEWORTHY

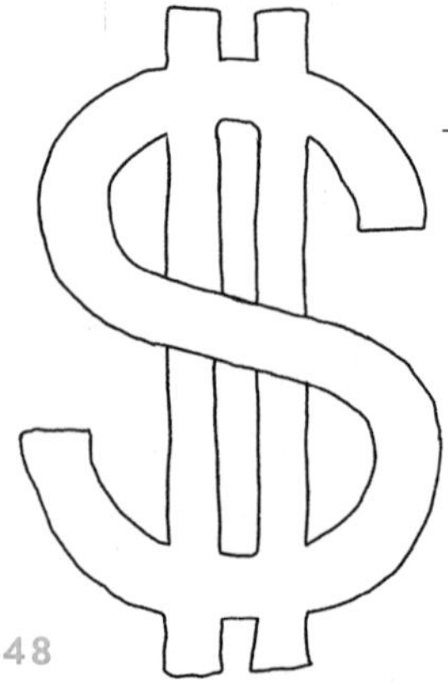

IT'S MY JAM

Obsessed

Love

Like

Meh

Pass

THINGS THAT KEEP ME UP AT NIGHT

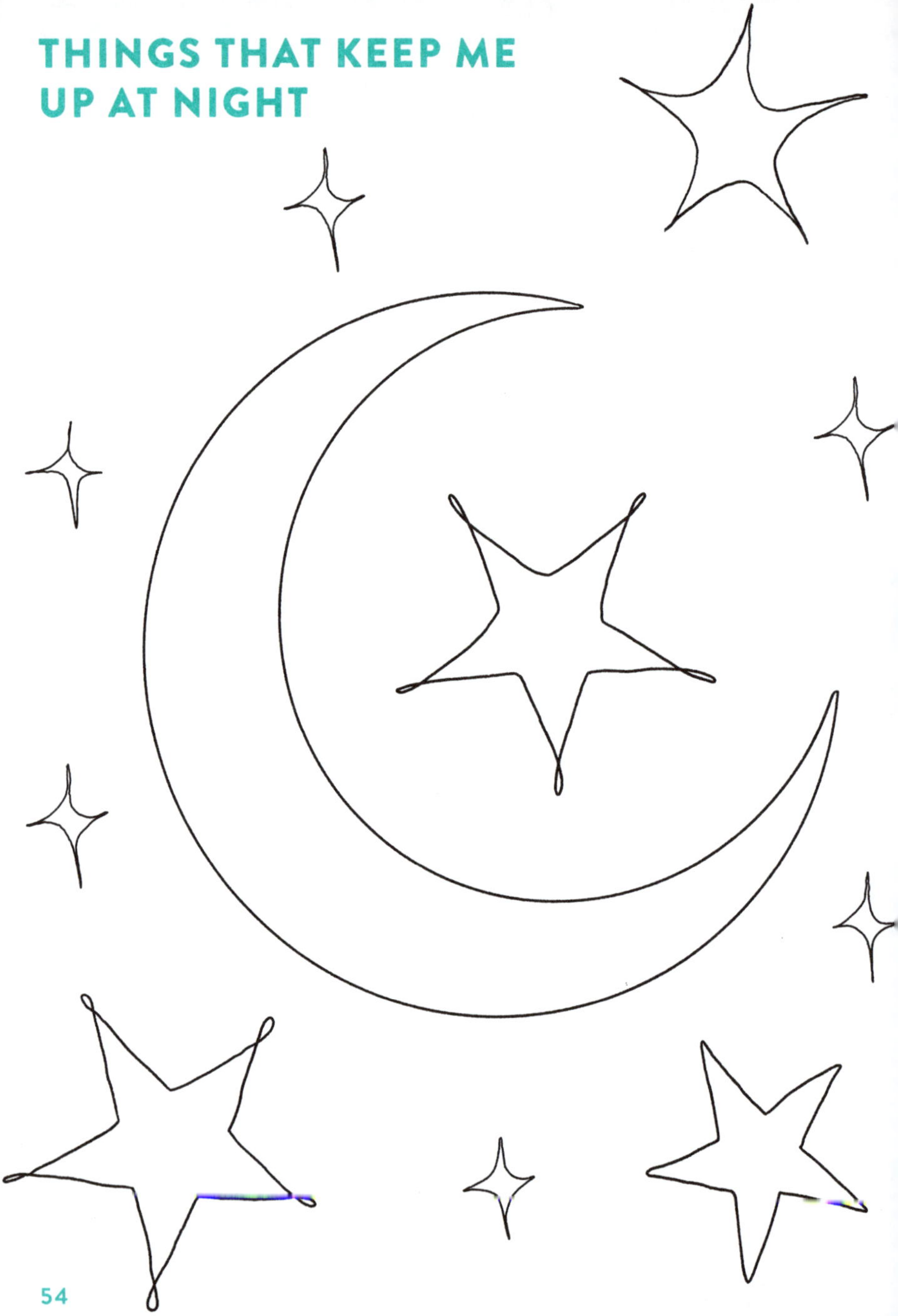

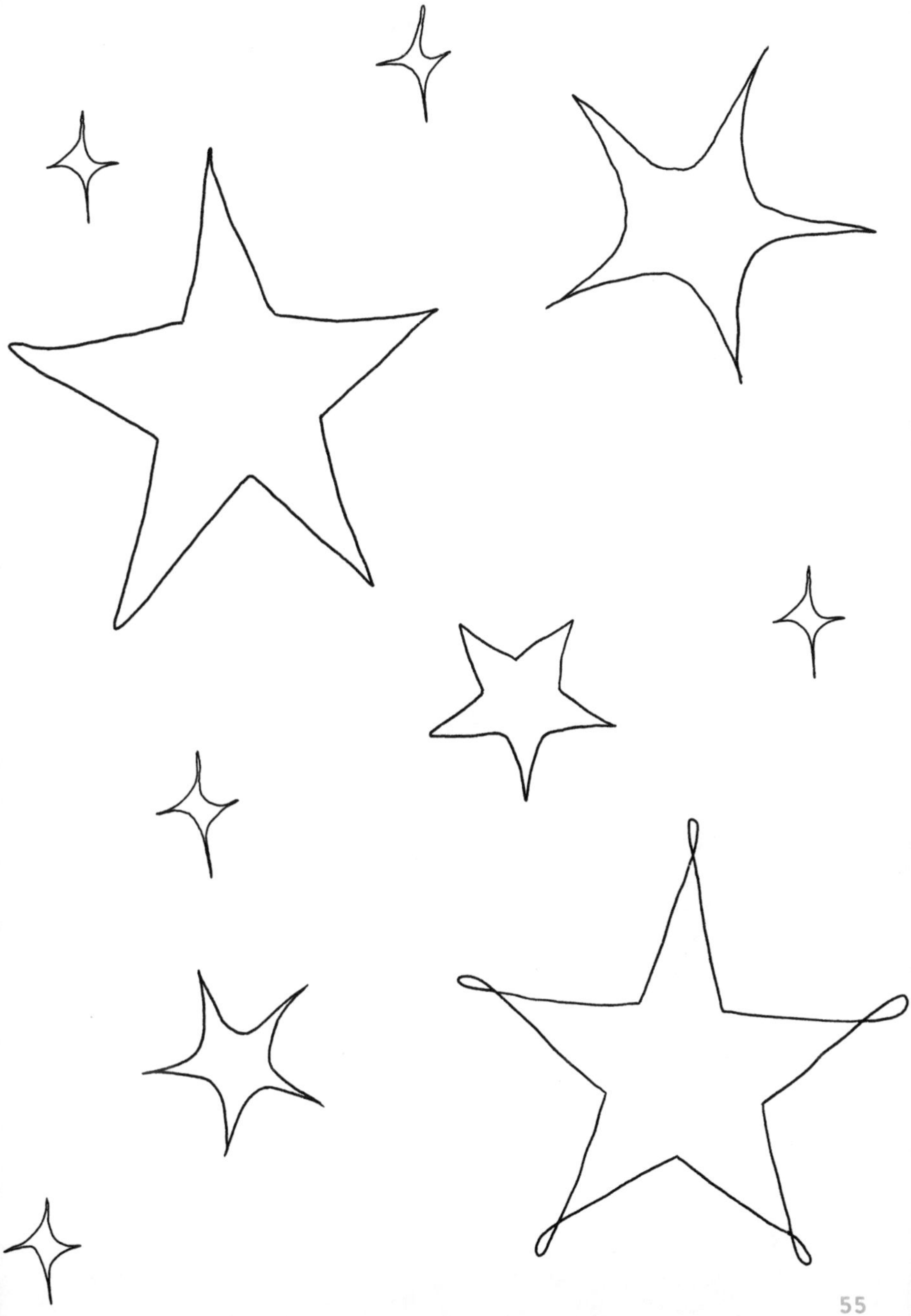

SHOWER THOUGHTS

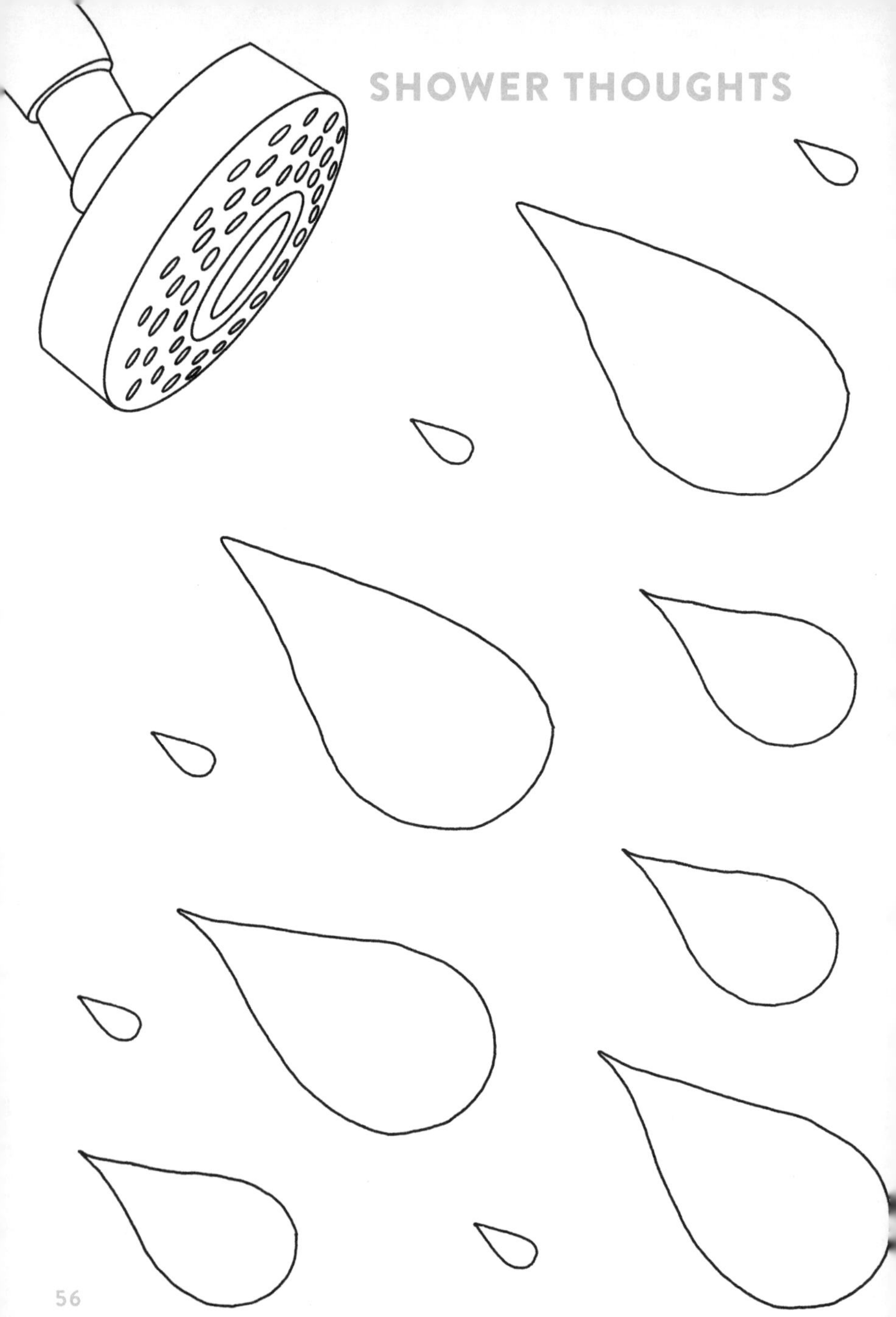

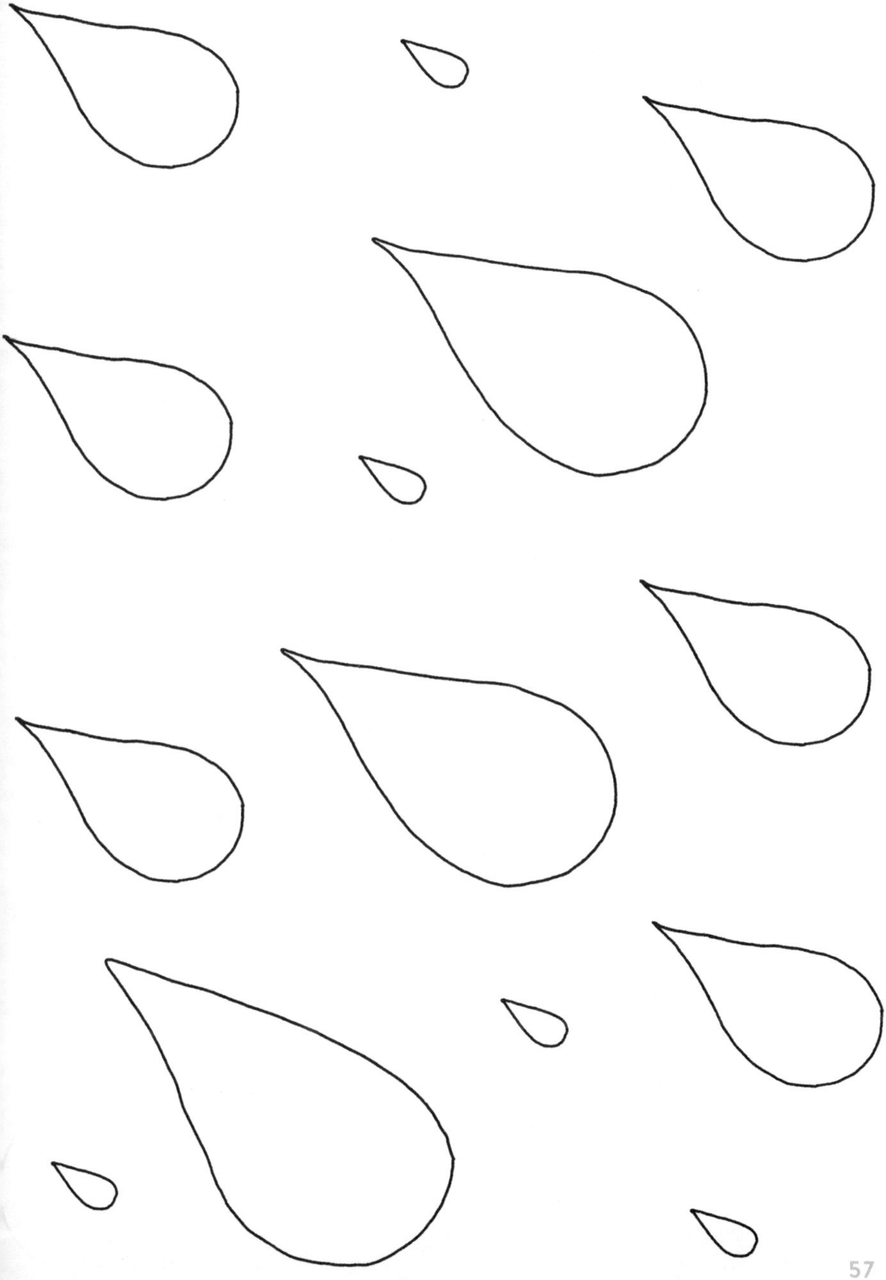

ME IRL

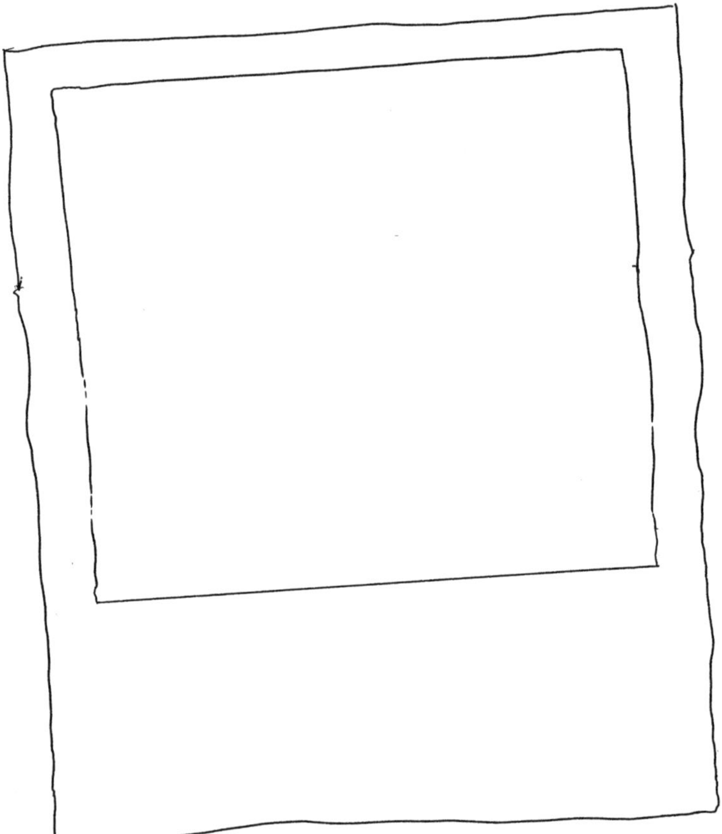

TIL: TODAY I LEARNED...

_____

_____

_____

_____

_____

_____

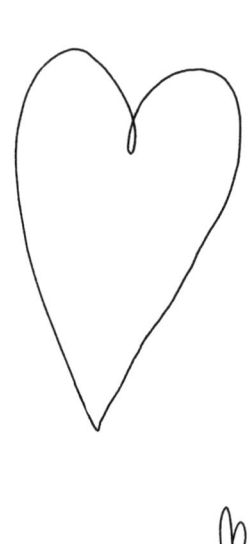

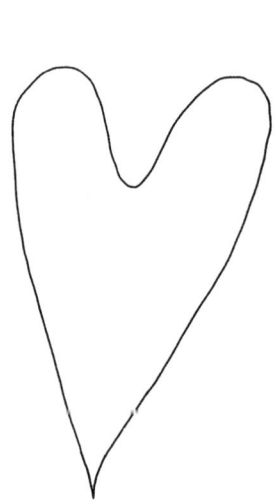

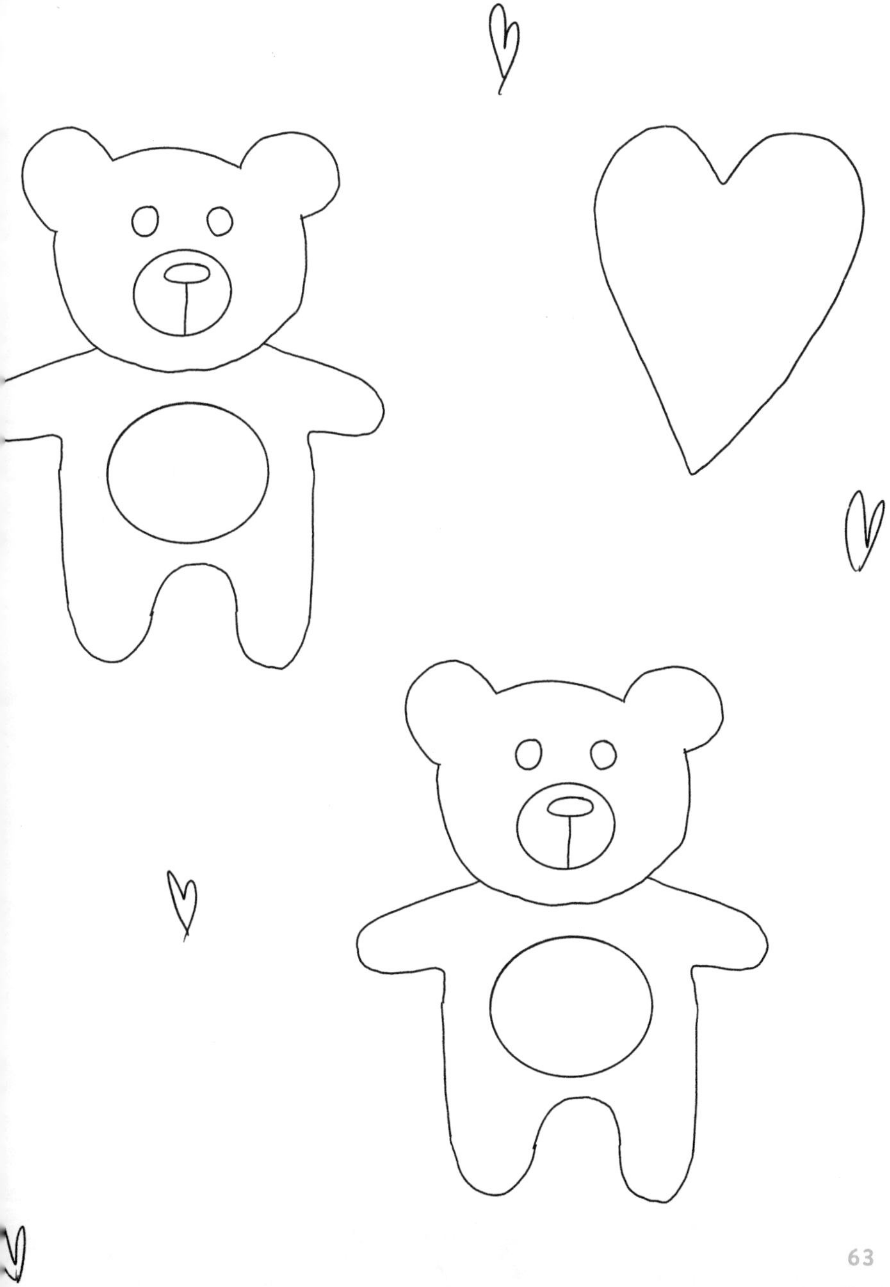

MY BEST FRIEND

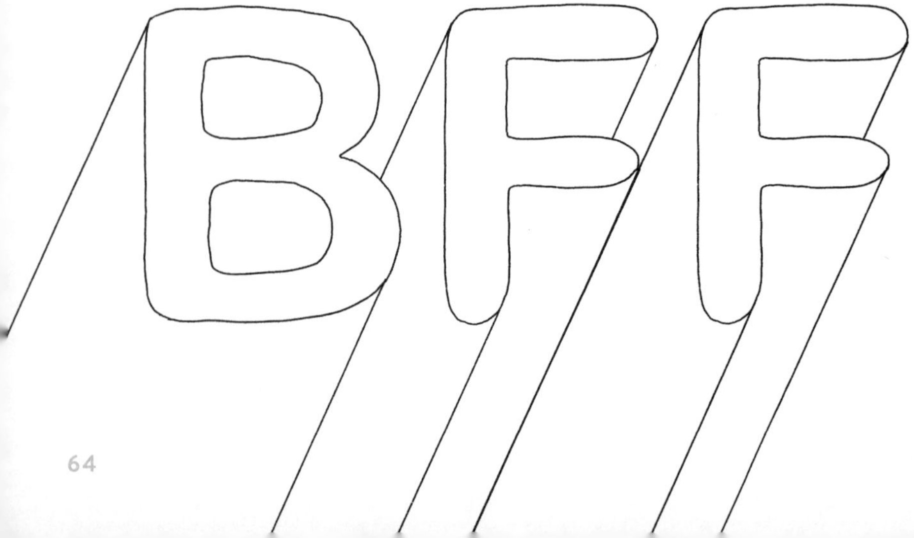
BFF

DETOXING WITH....

#GOALS

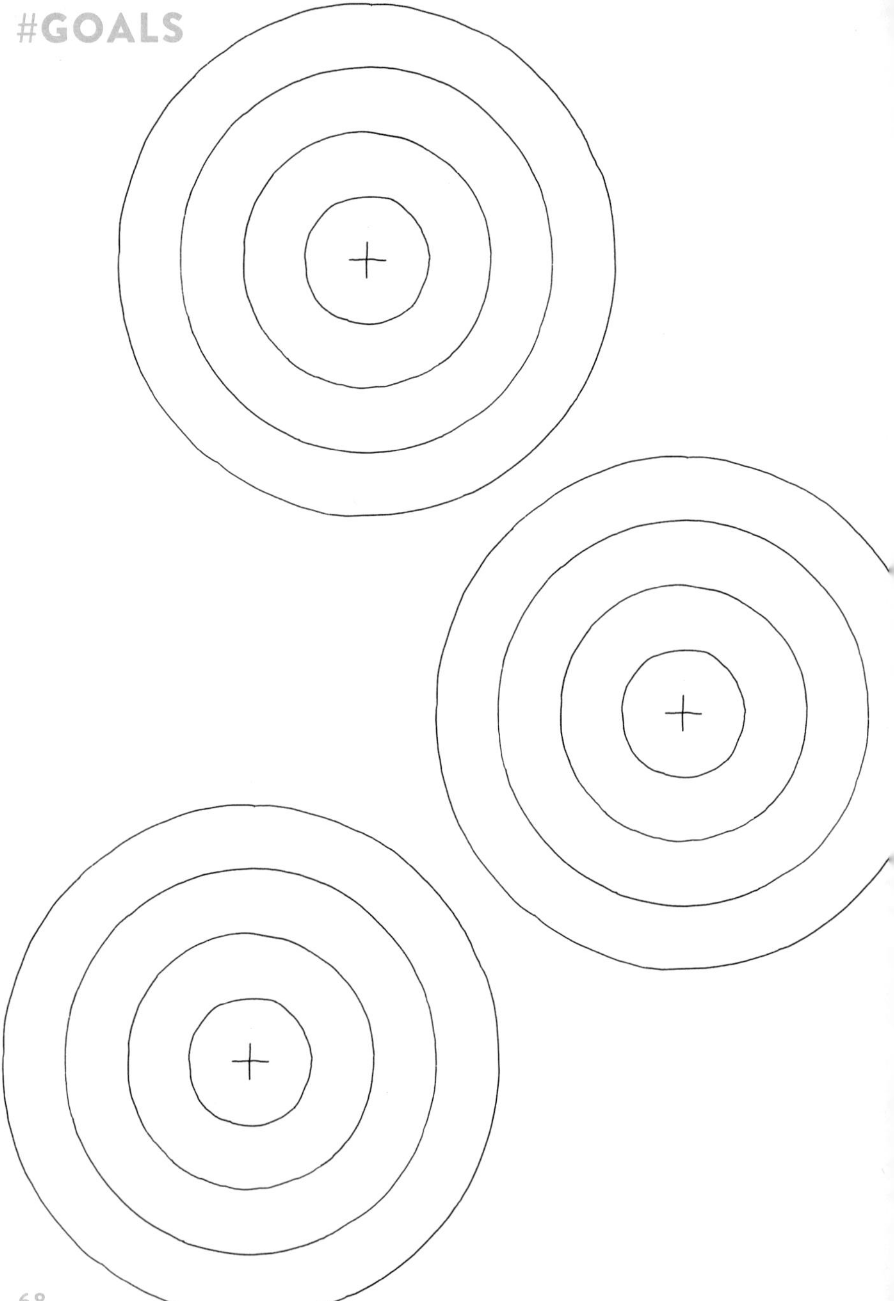

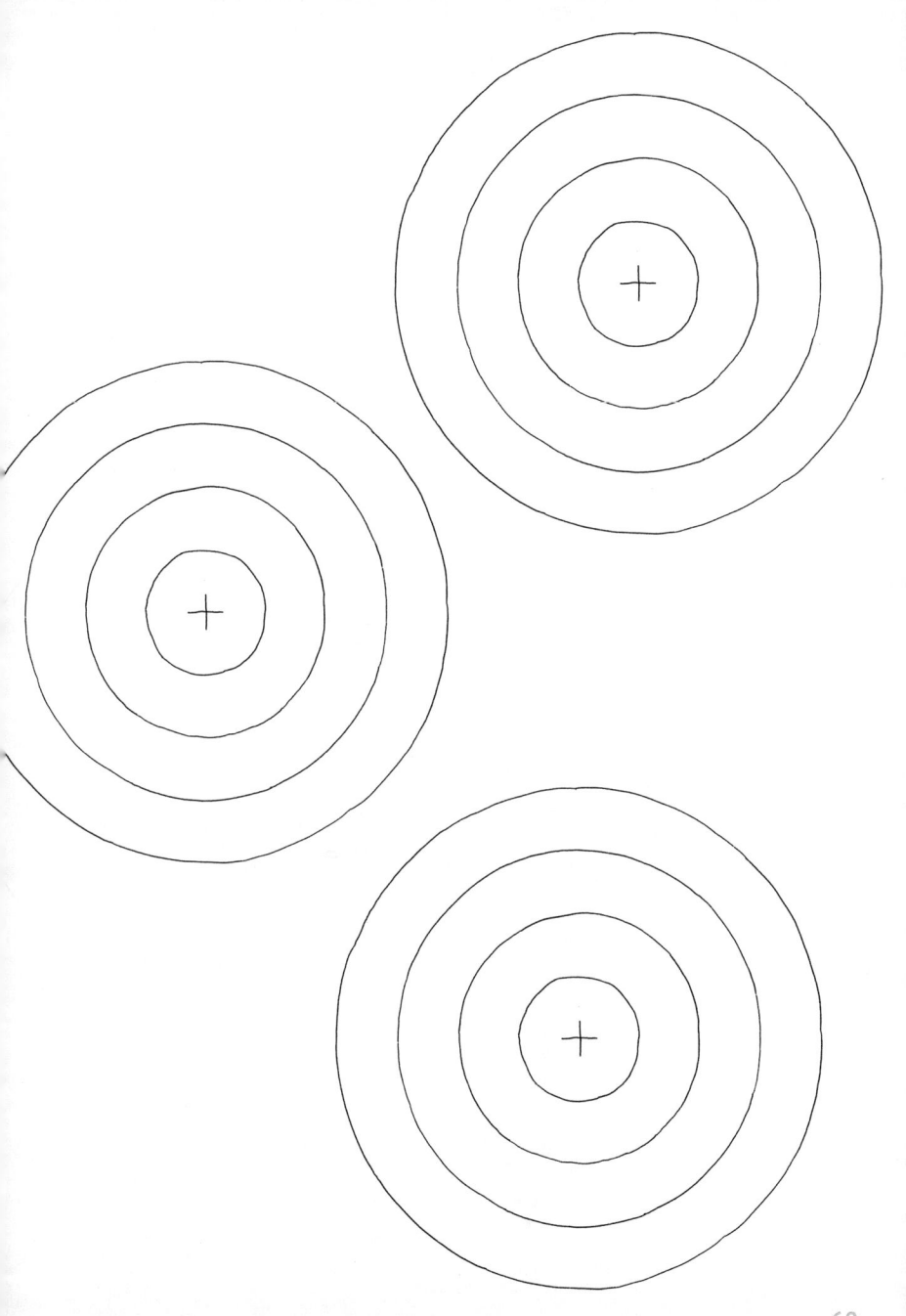

WHAT I'M WATCHING WHEN IT'S _____

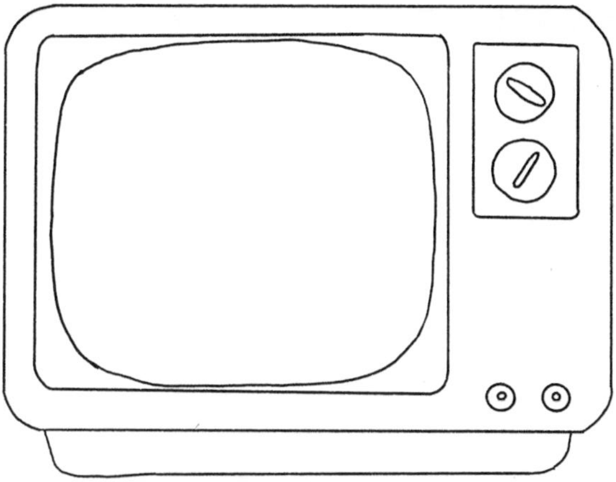
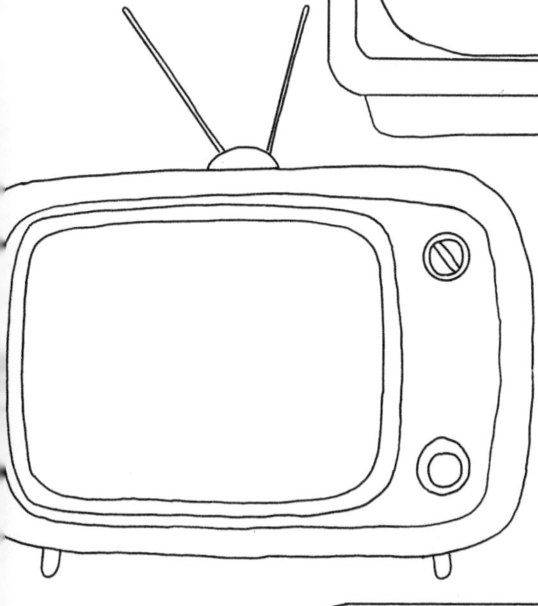
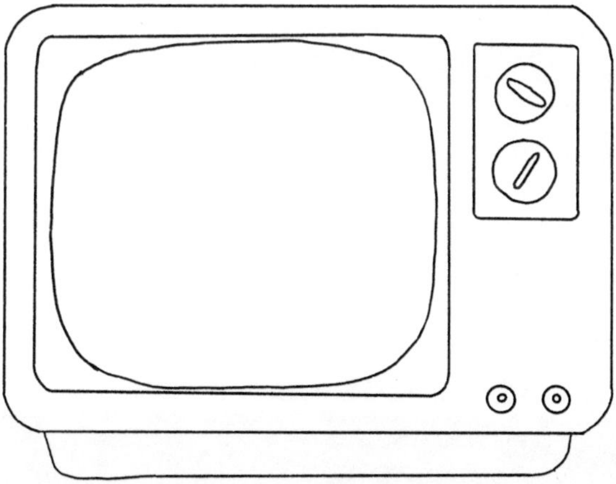

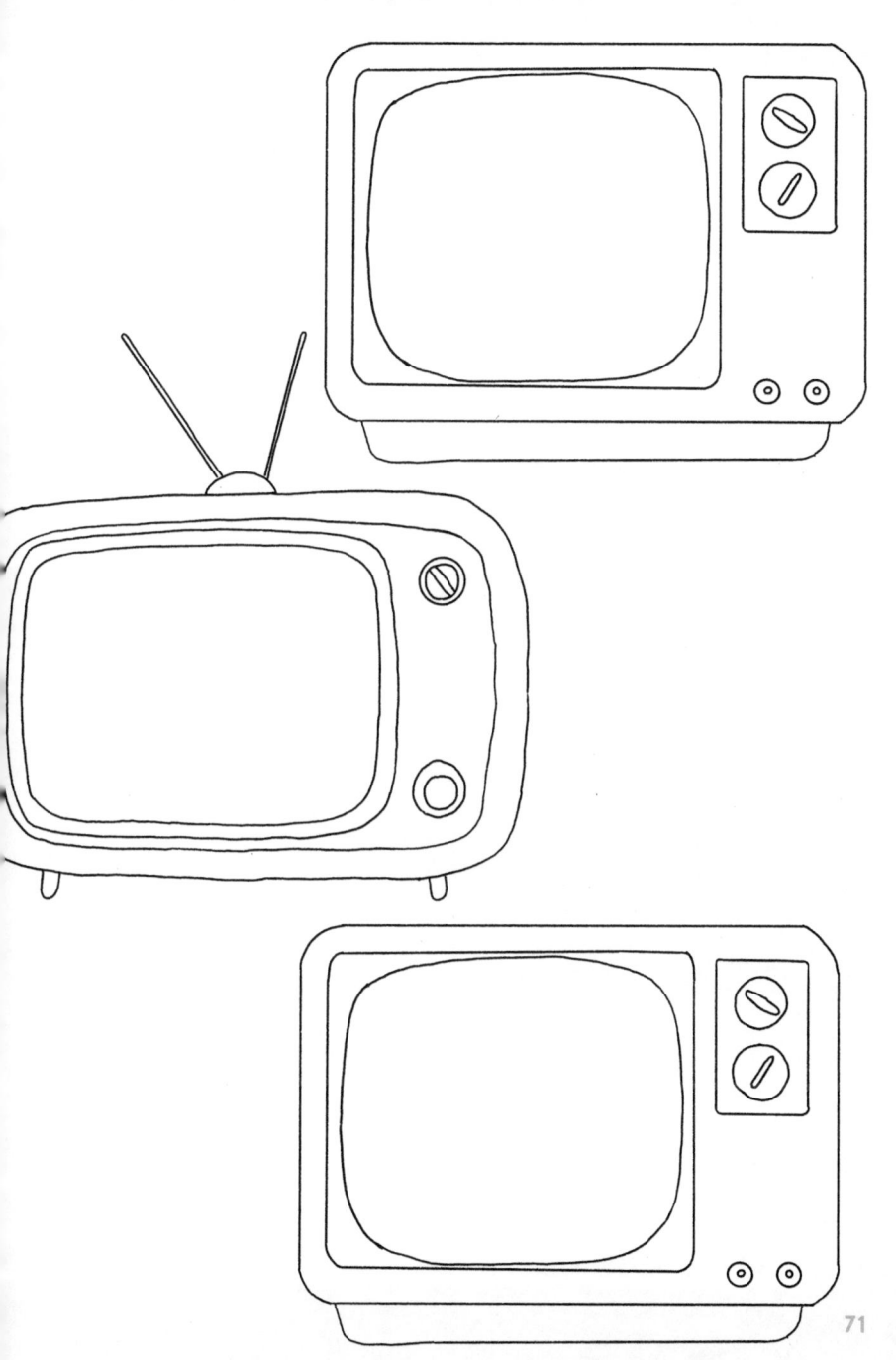

THINGS I LOW-KEY LOVE

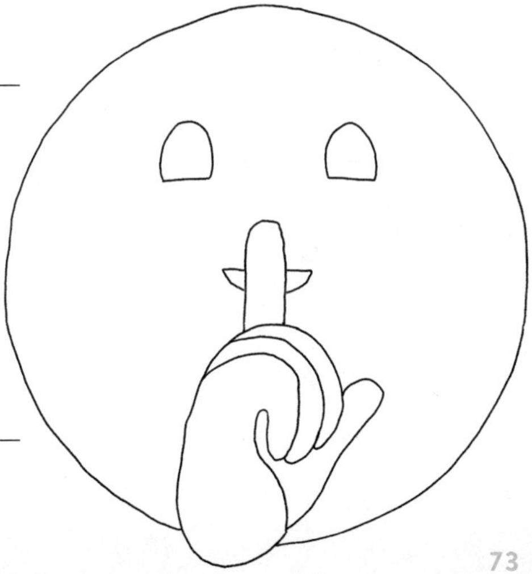

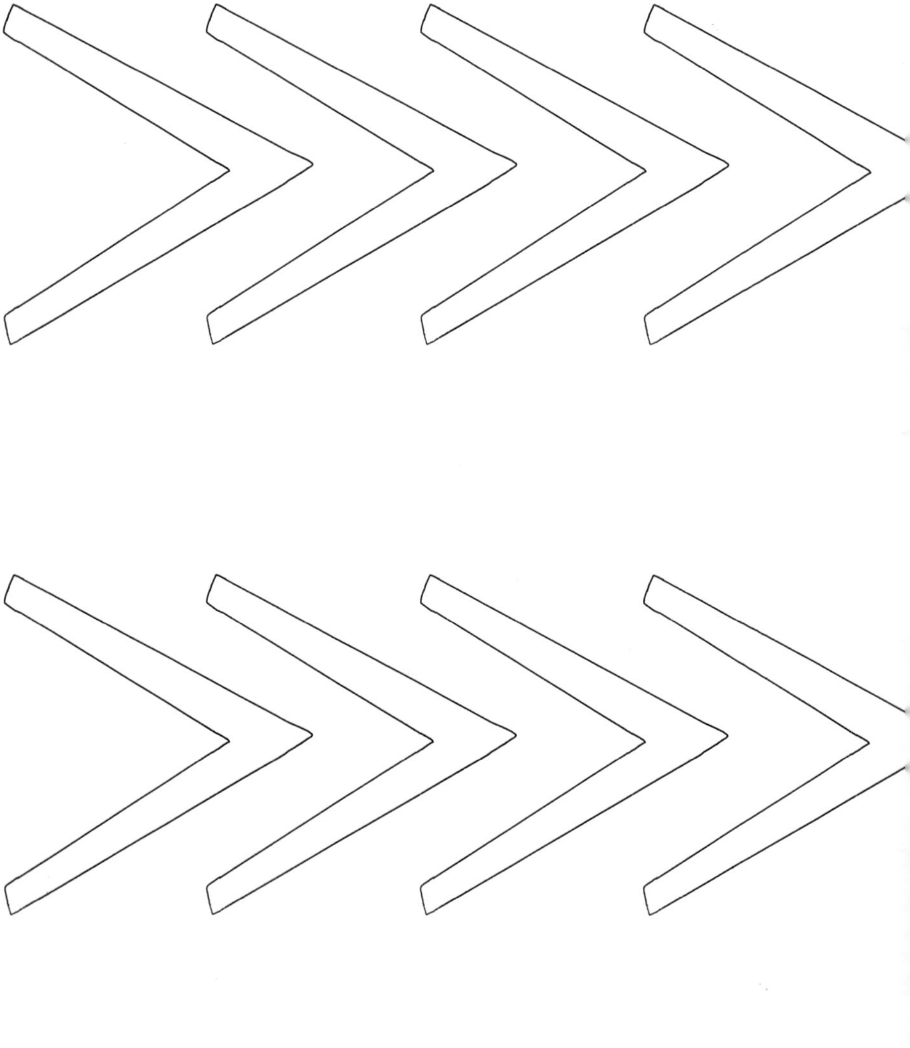

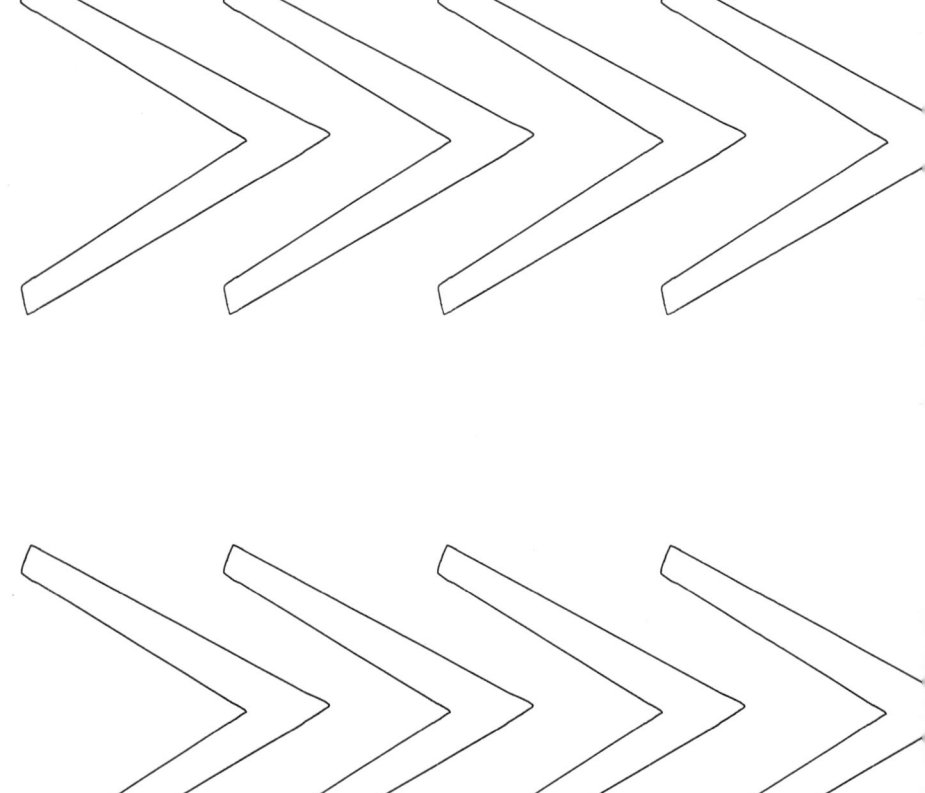

RANDOM FACTS

Did you know?

THIS HAD ME DEAD

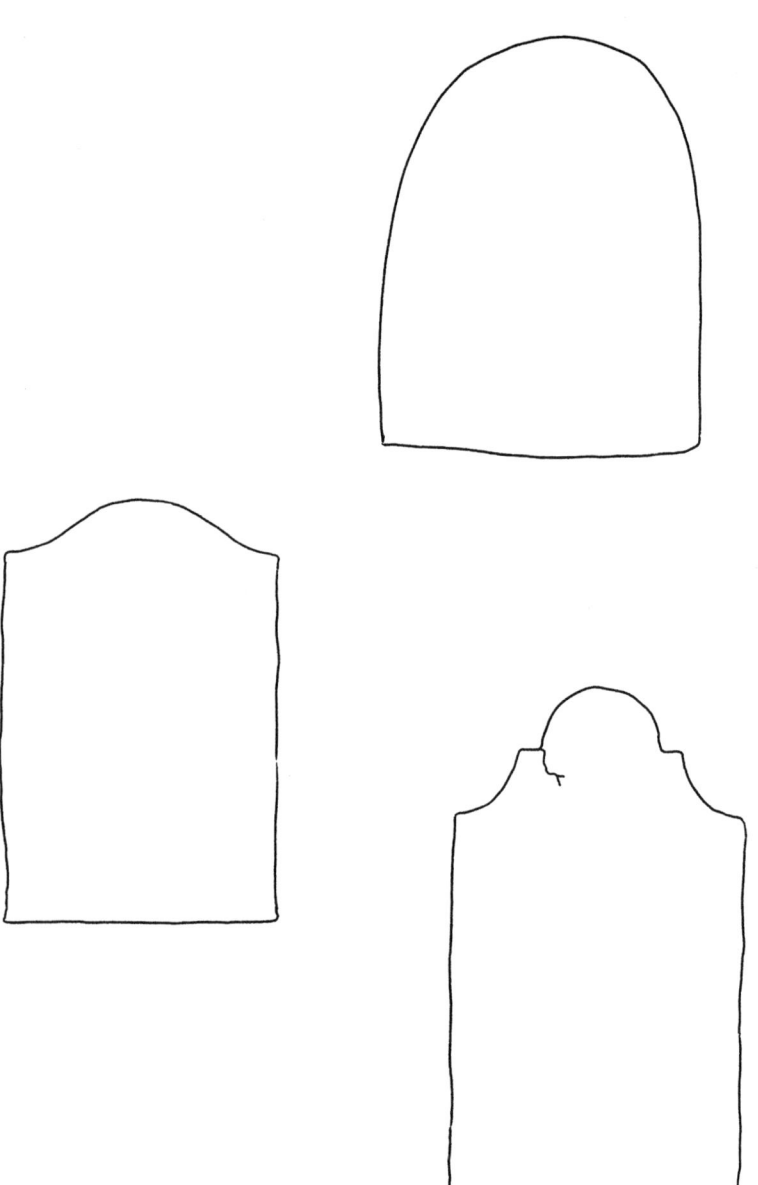

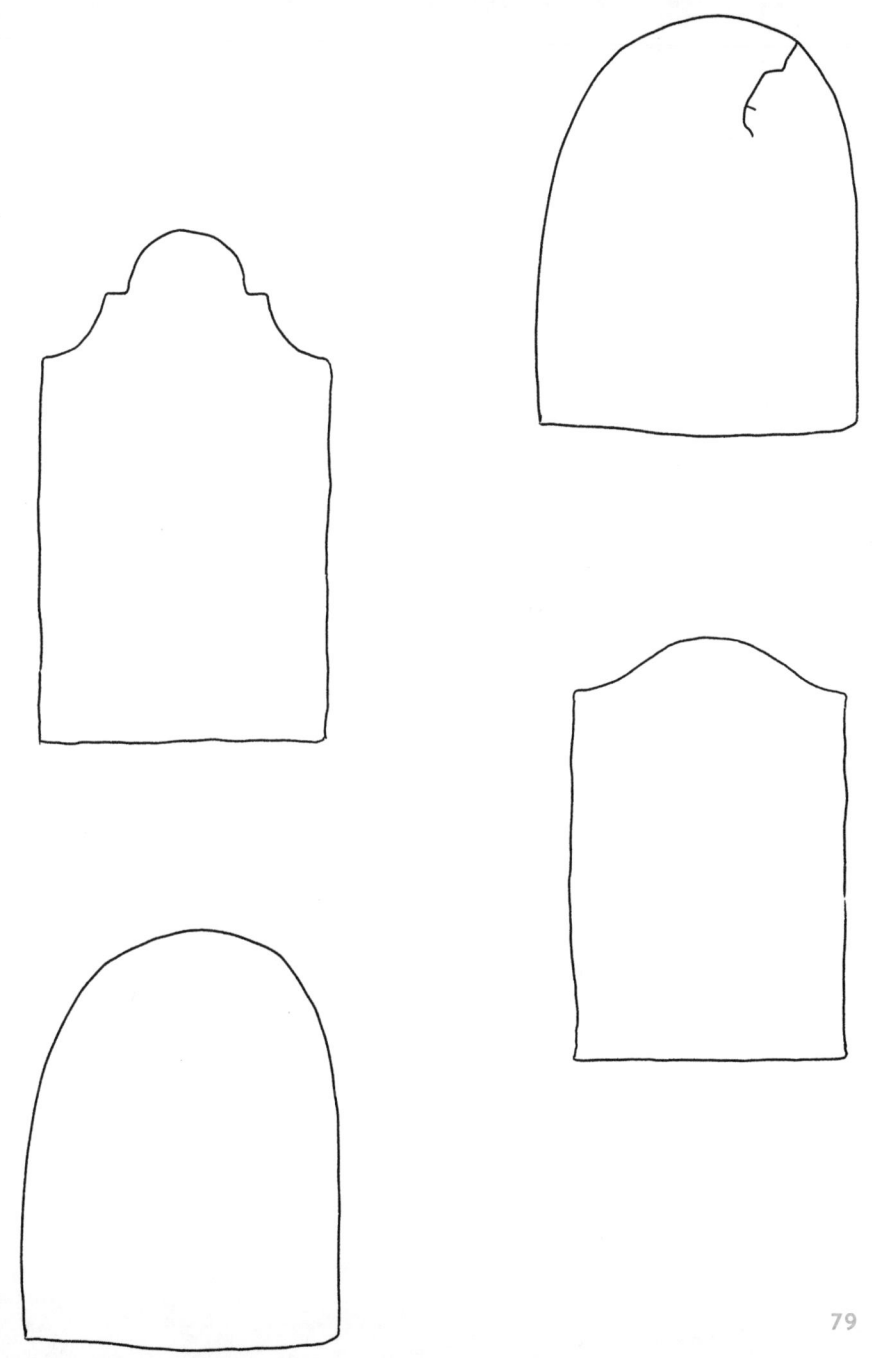

VIBES

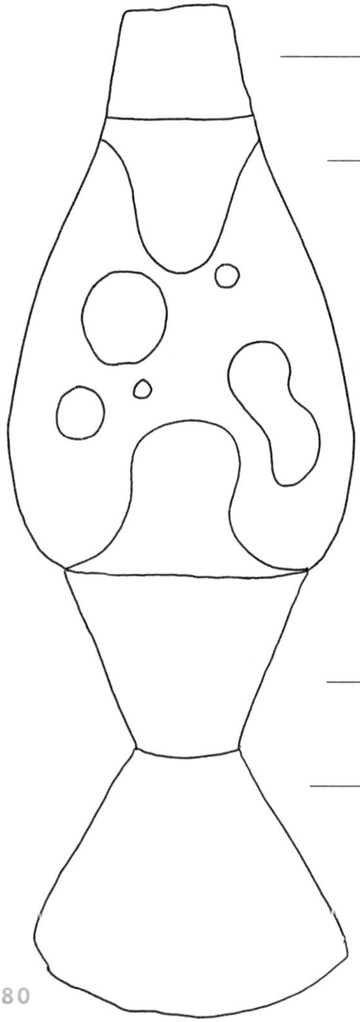

THINGS THAT ARE SUS

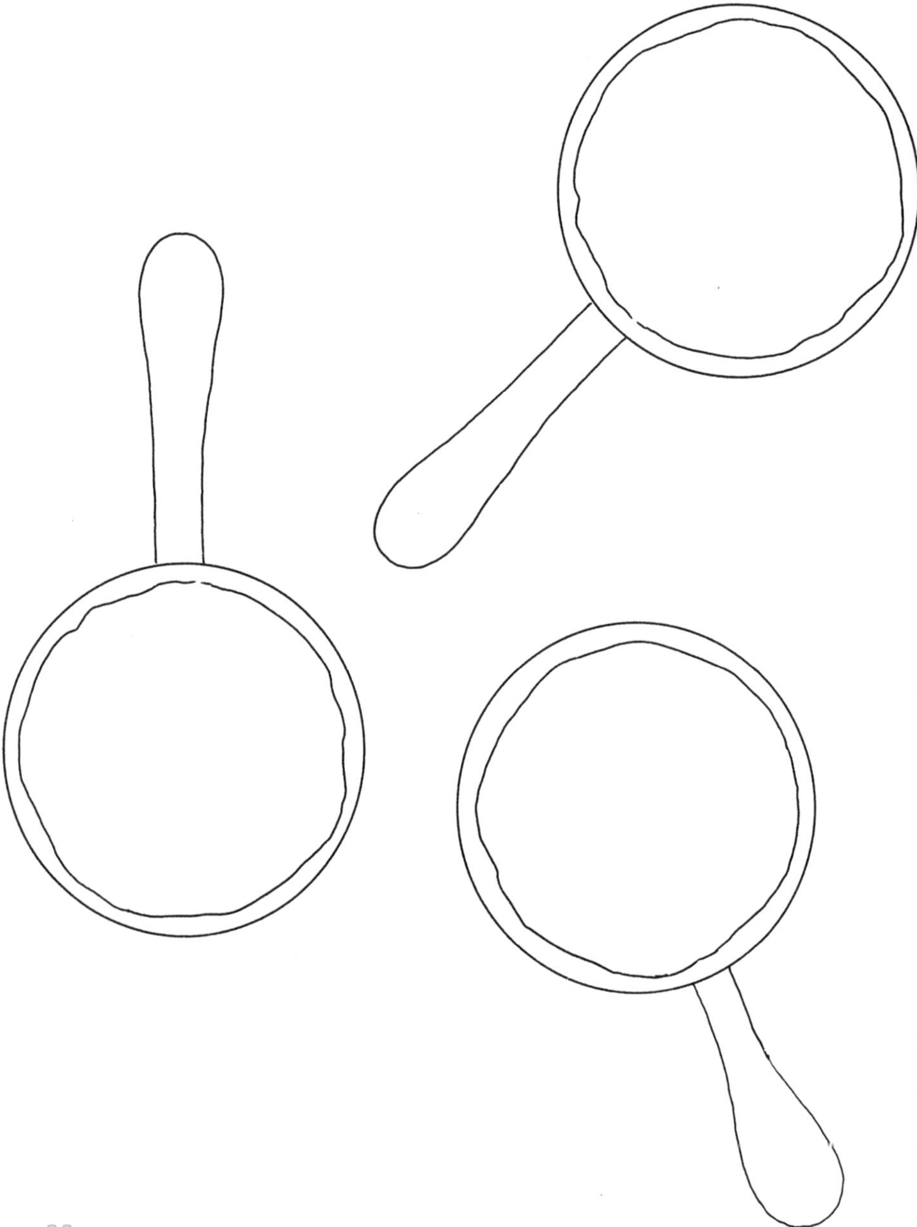

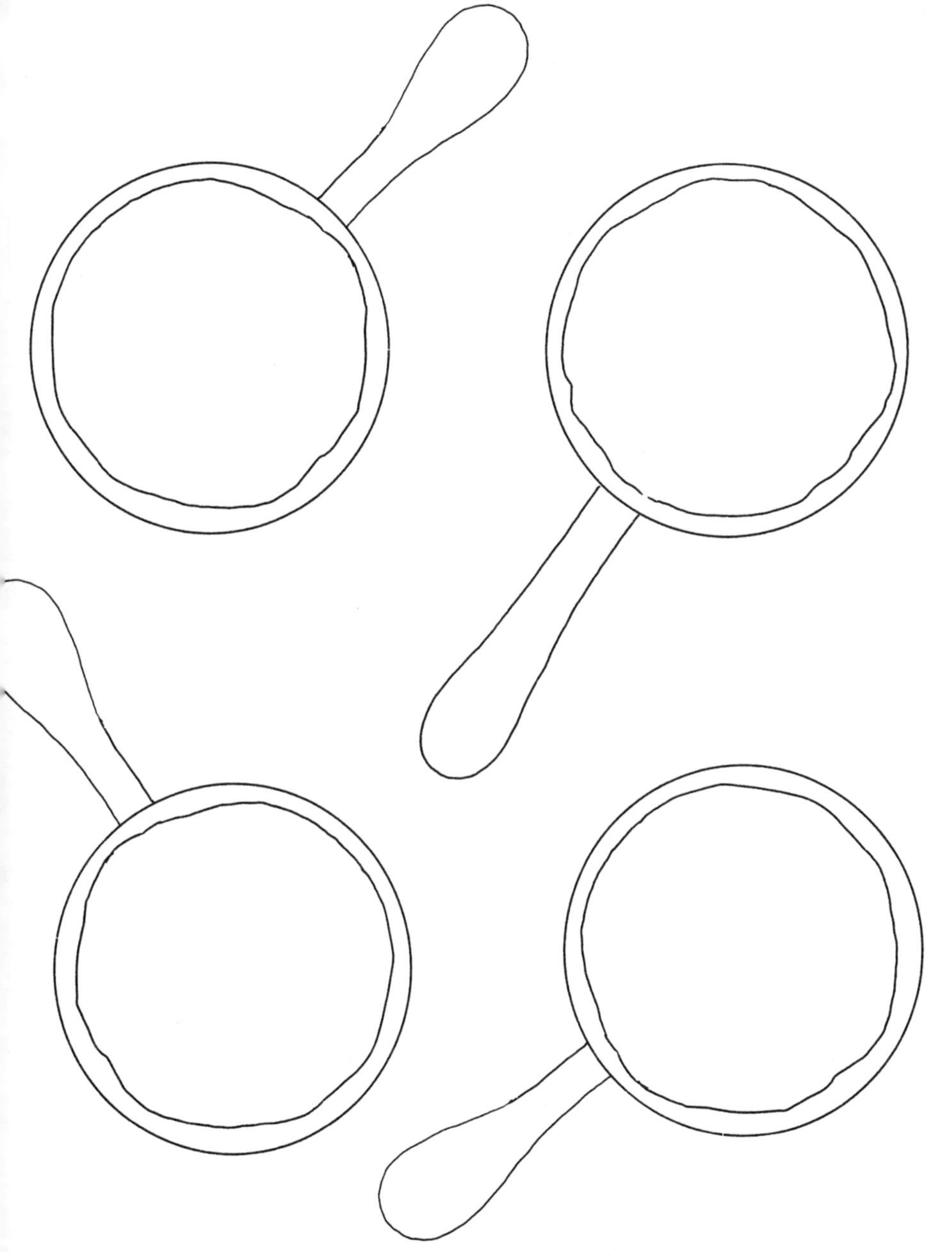

IF MY PET COULD TALK, THEY'D SAY...

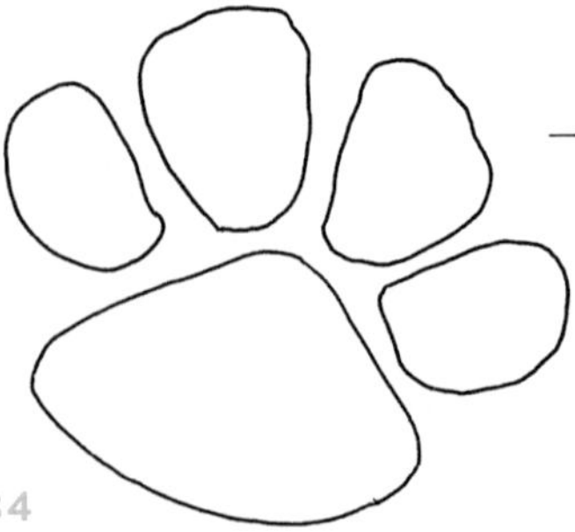

QUOTES TO LIVE BY

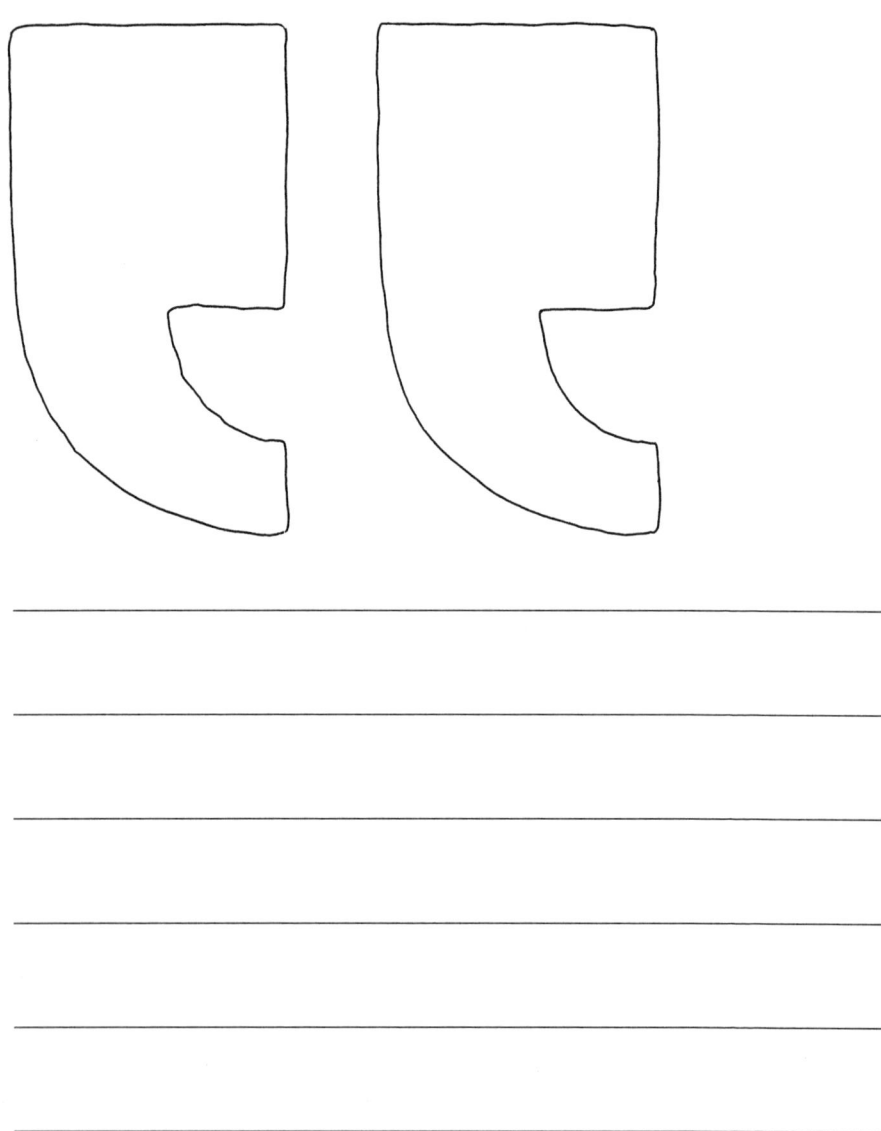

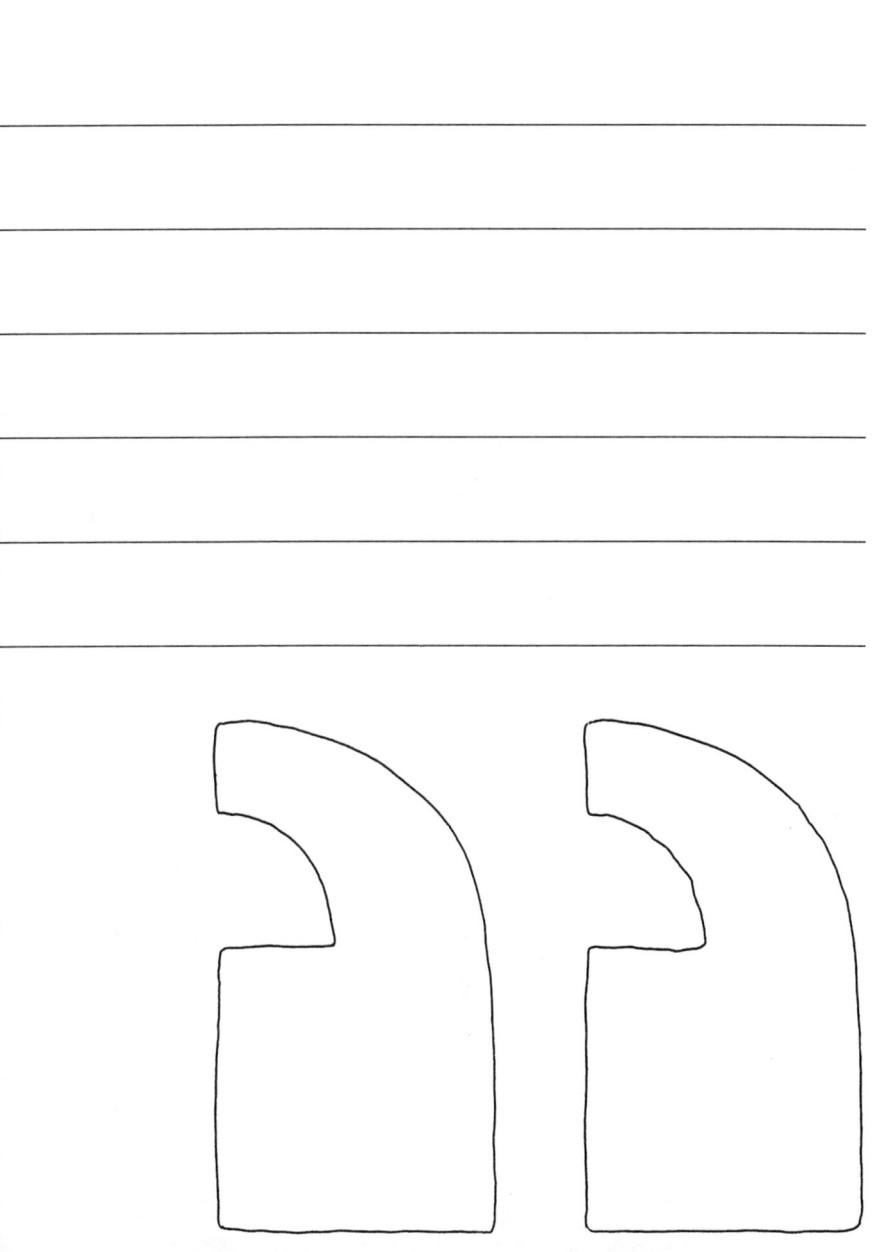

I'M TOTALLY EXTRA ABOUT...

_____

_____

_____

_____

_____

_____

#FINDS

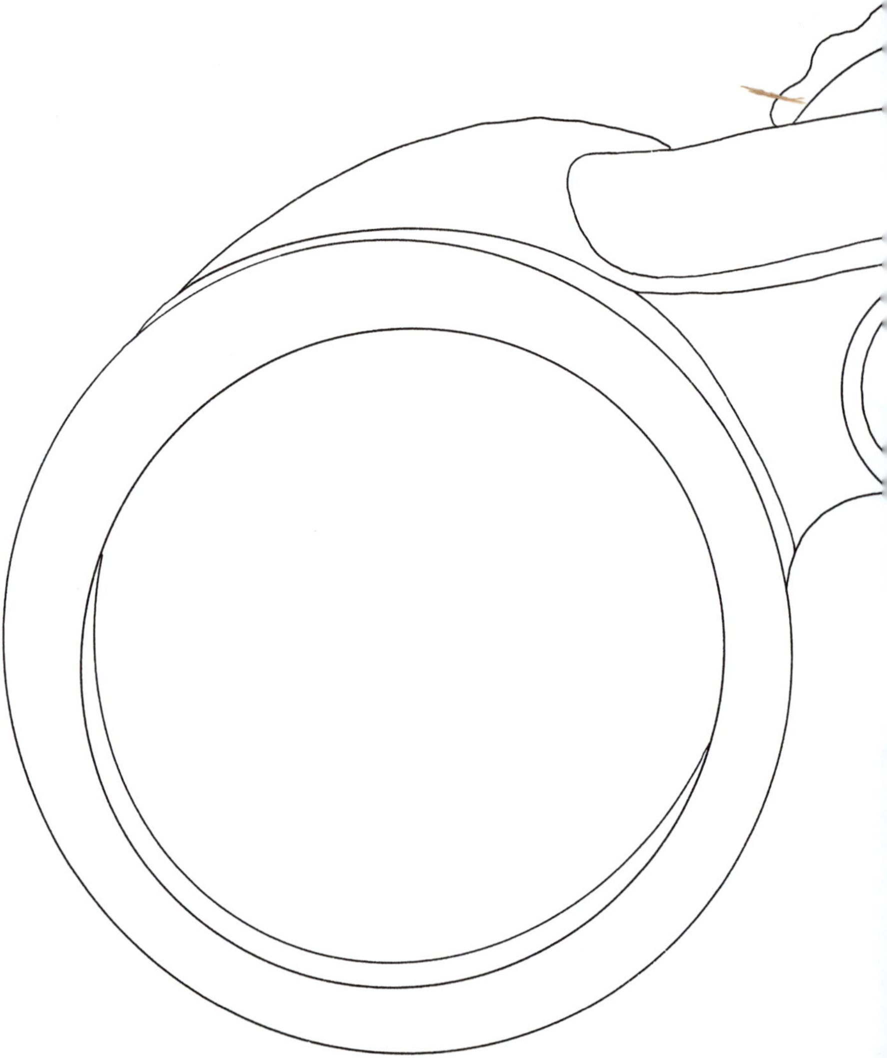

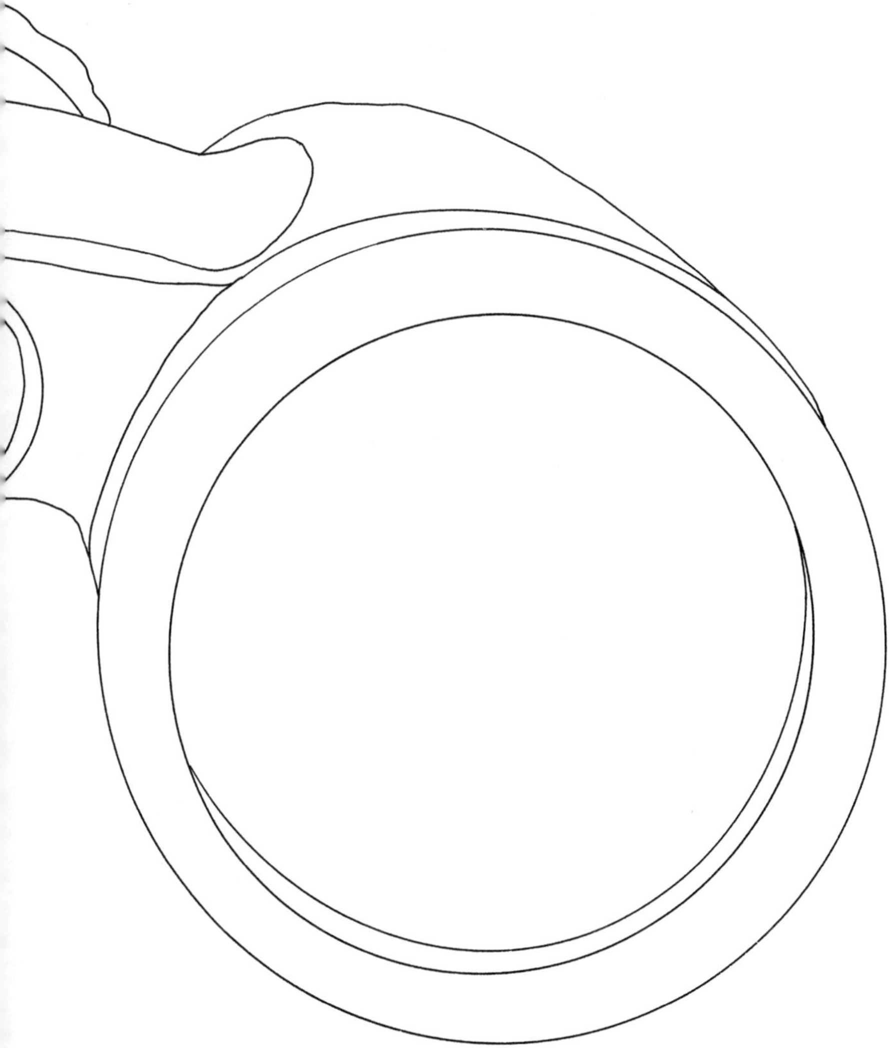

PUT A FINGER DOWN IF...

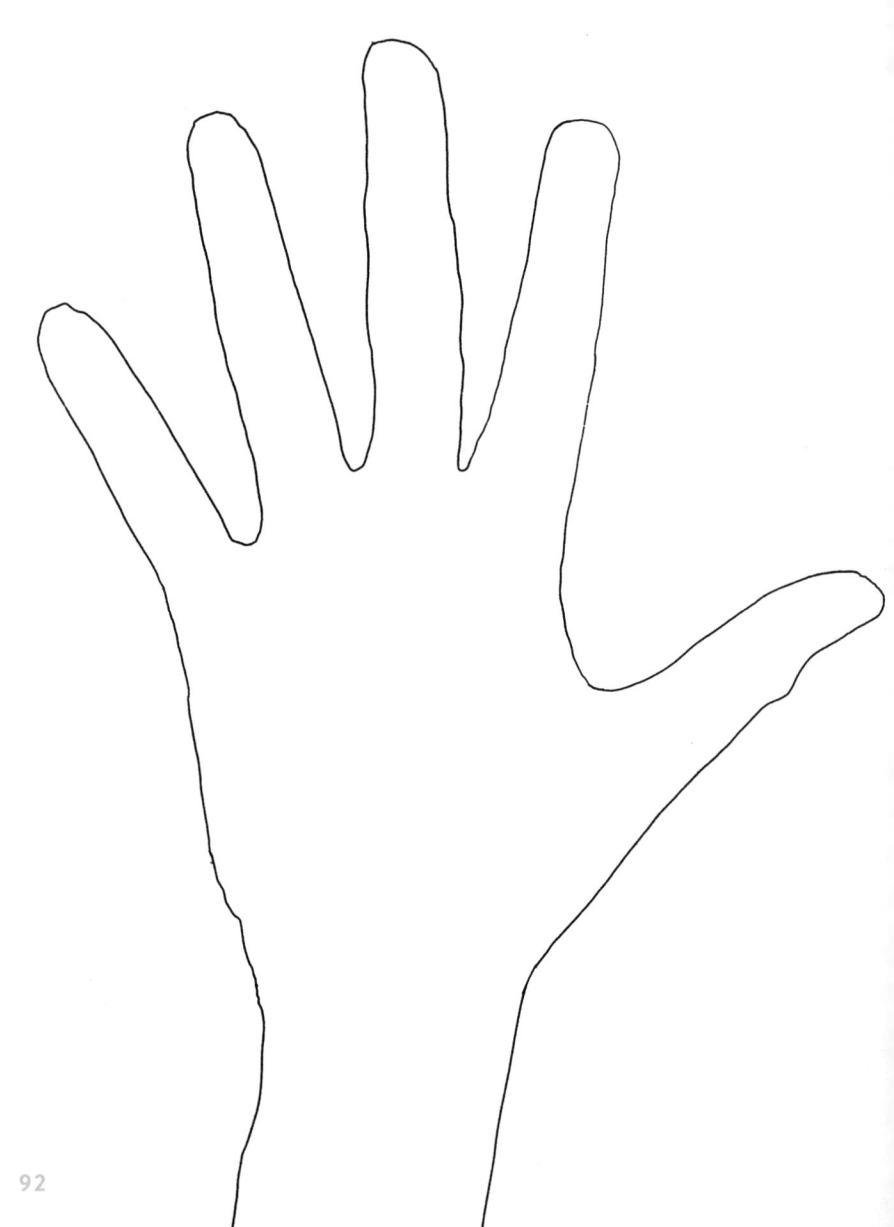

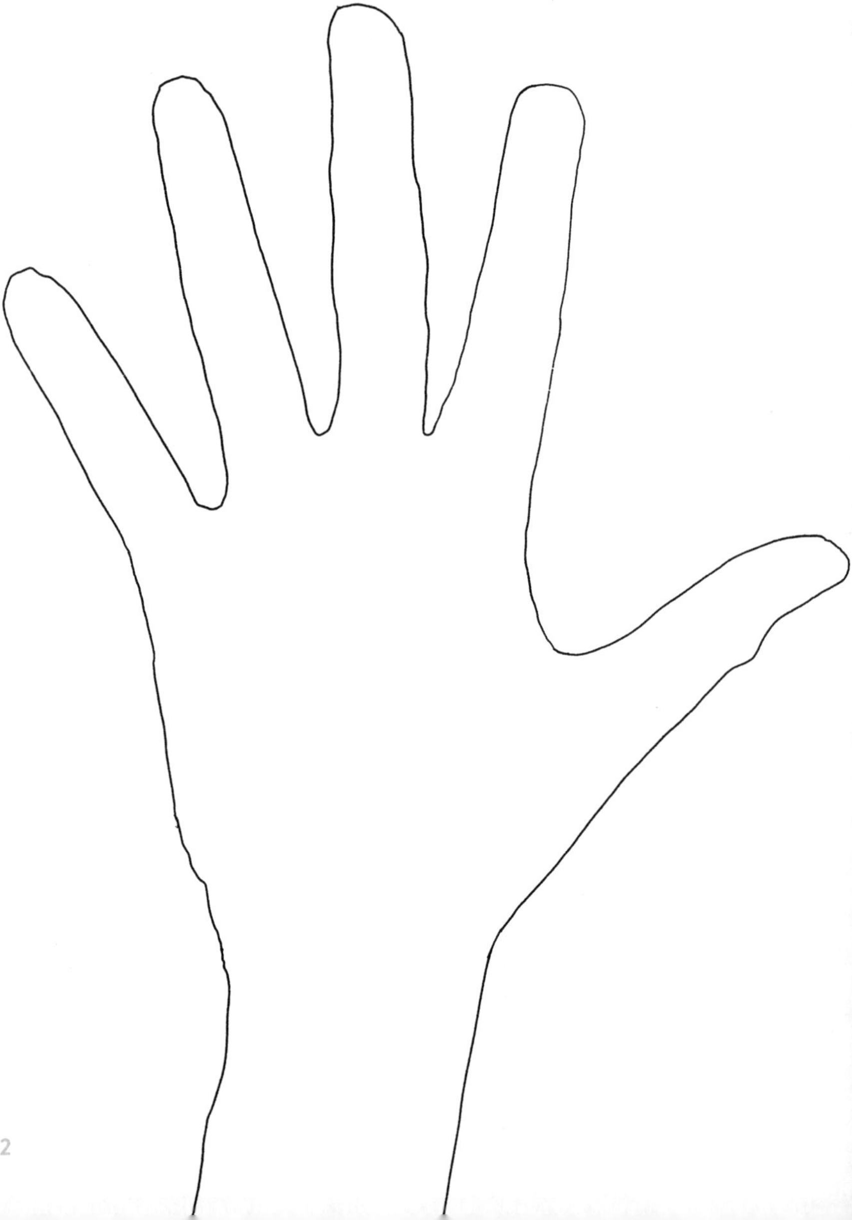

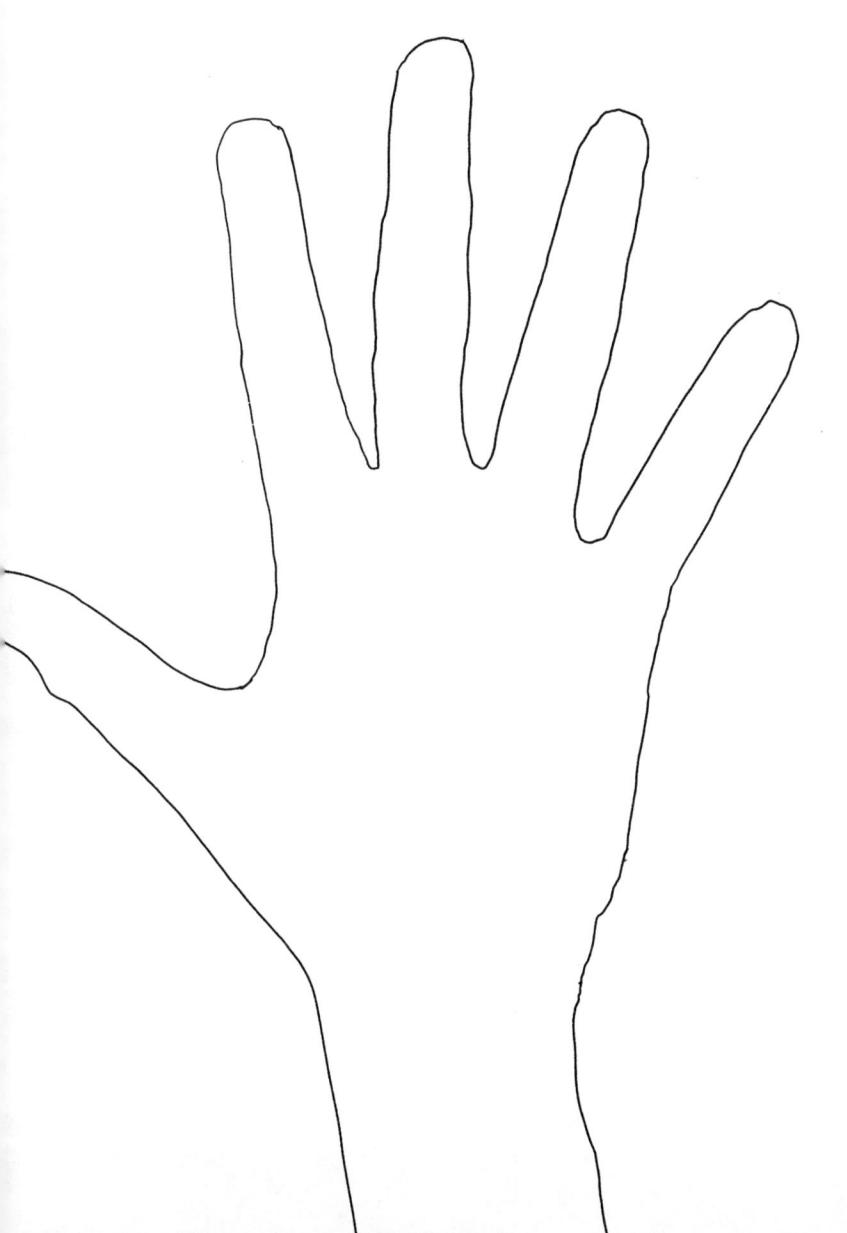

NOW LOOK AT THIS...

THE GOAT

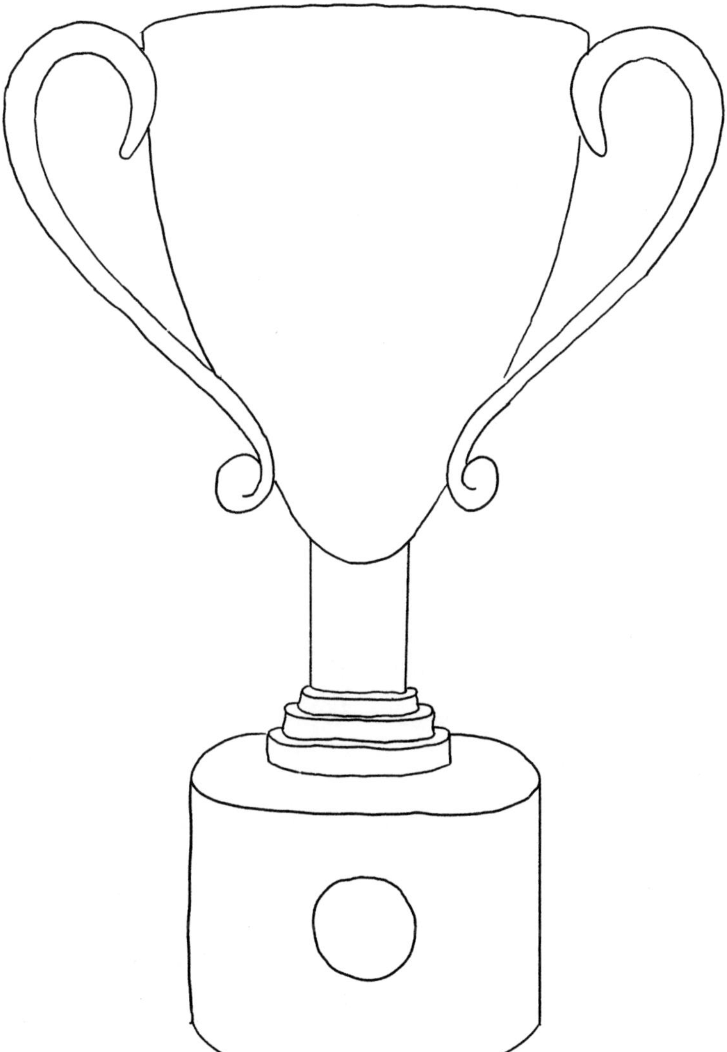

THINGS I NEVER WANT TO END

10 REASONS WHY ______________ IS THE BEST!

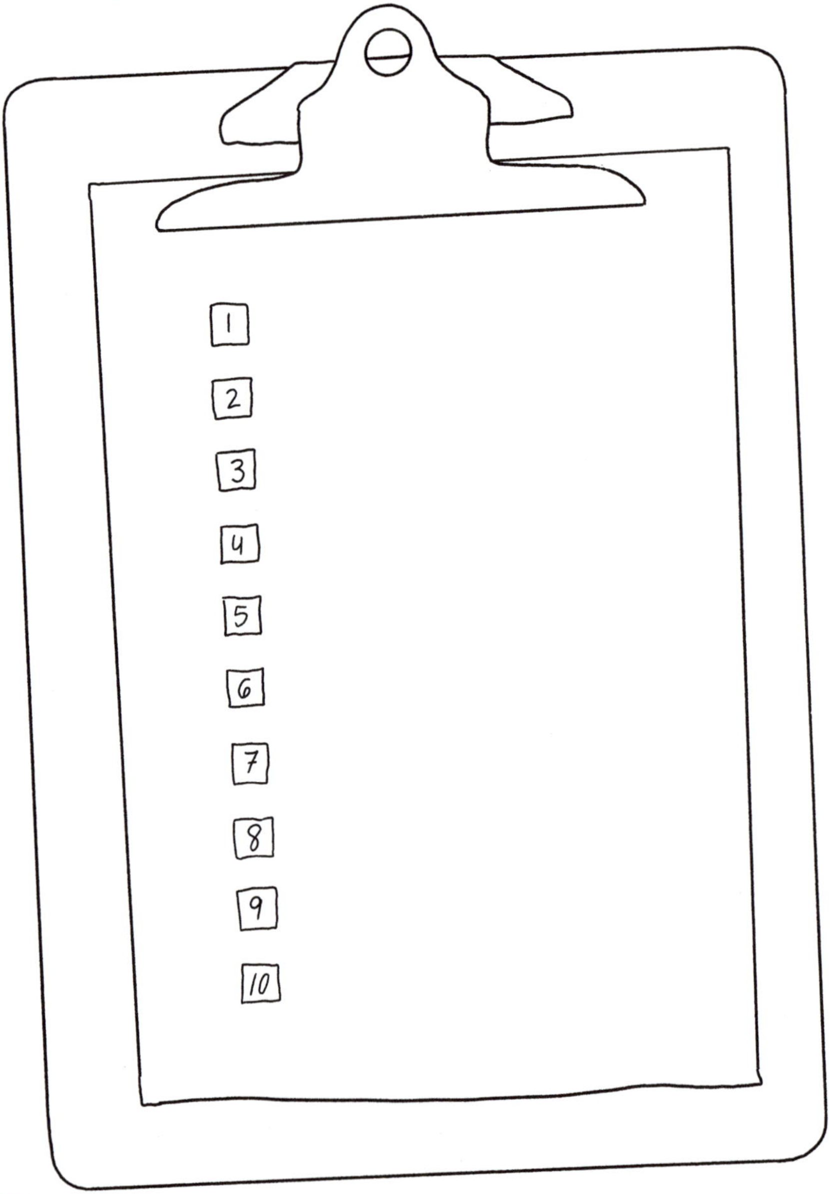

1
2
3
4
5
6
7
8
9
10

10 REASONS WHY ______________________ IS THE WORST!

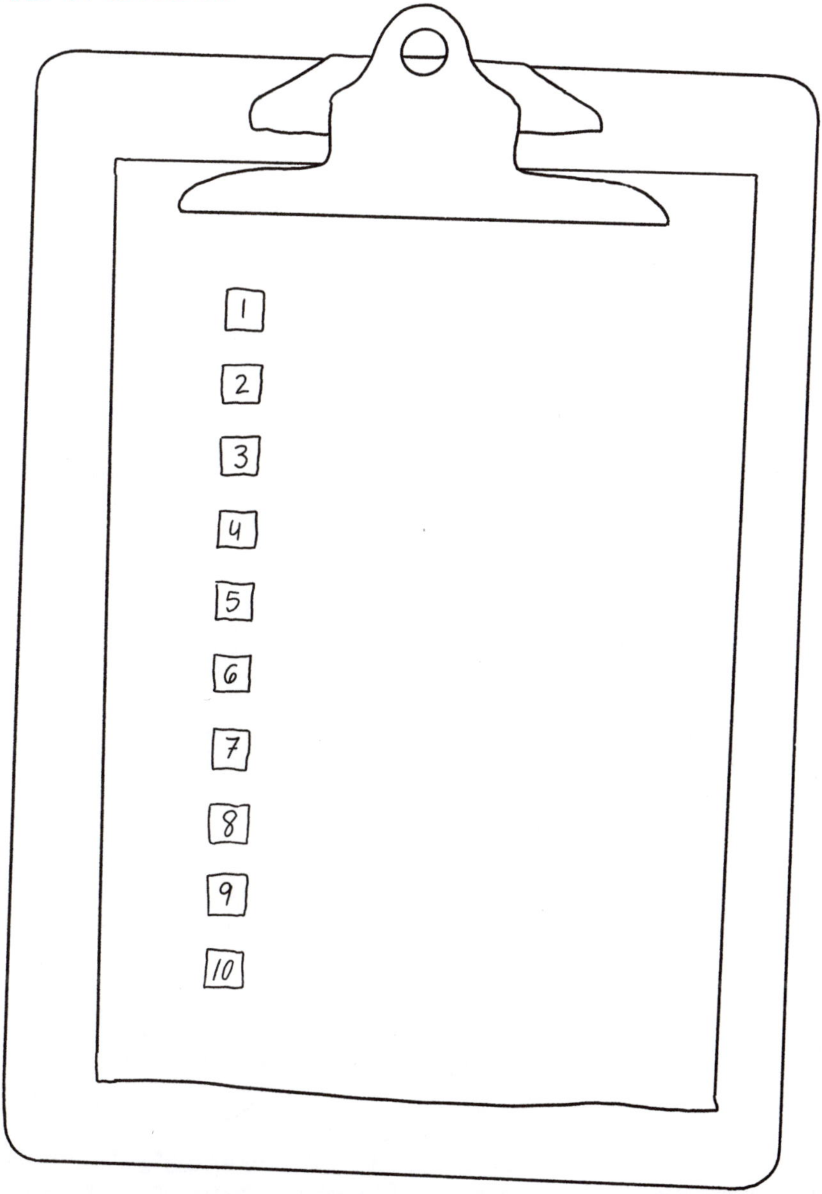
1
2
3
4
5
6
7
8
9
10

A FAN LETTER TO THE THING I LOVE THE MOST

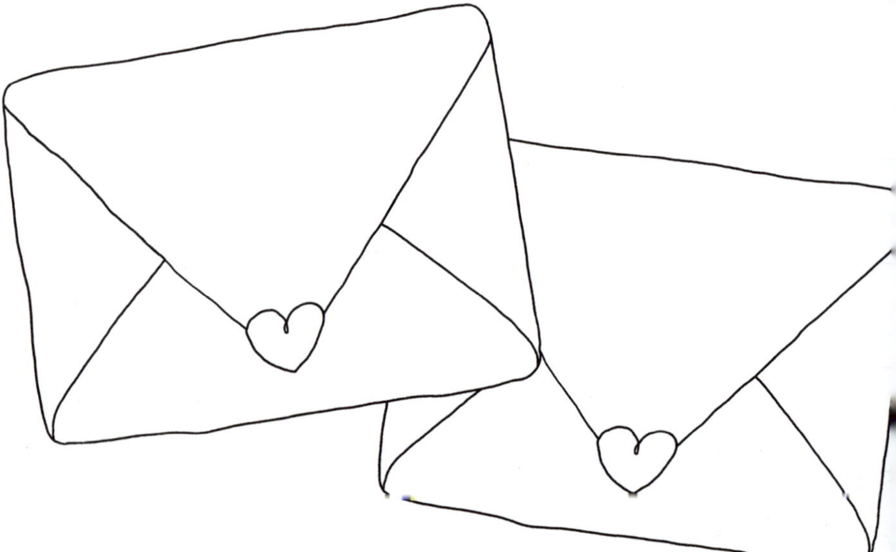

#STYLE

#style

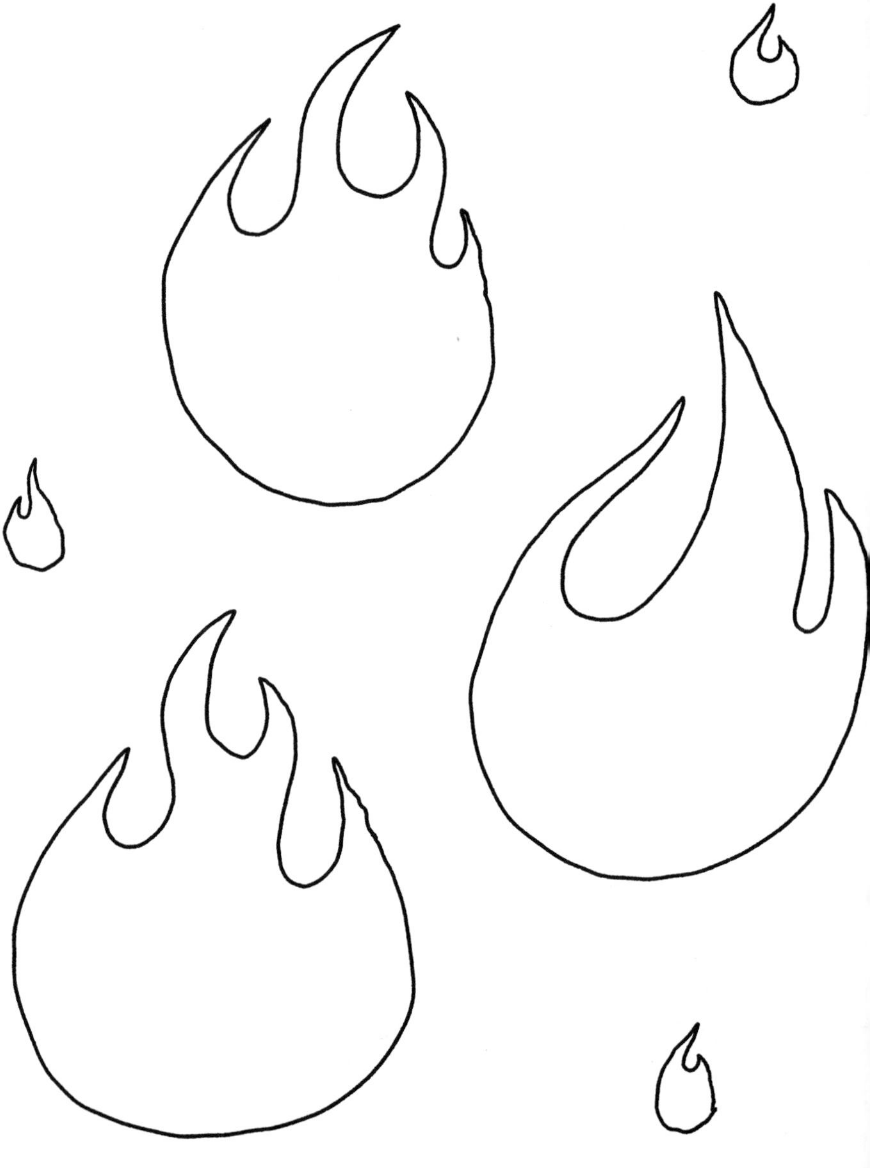

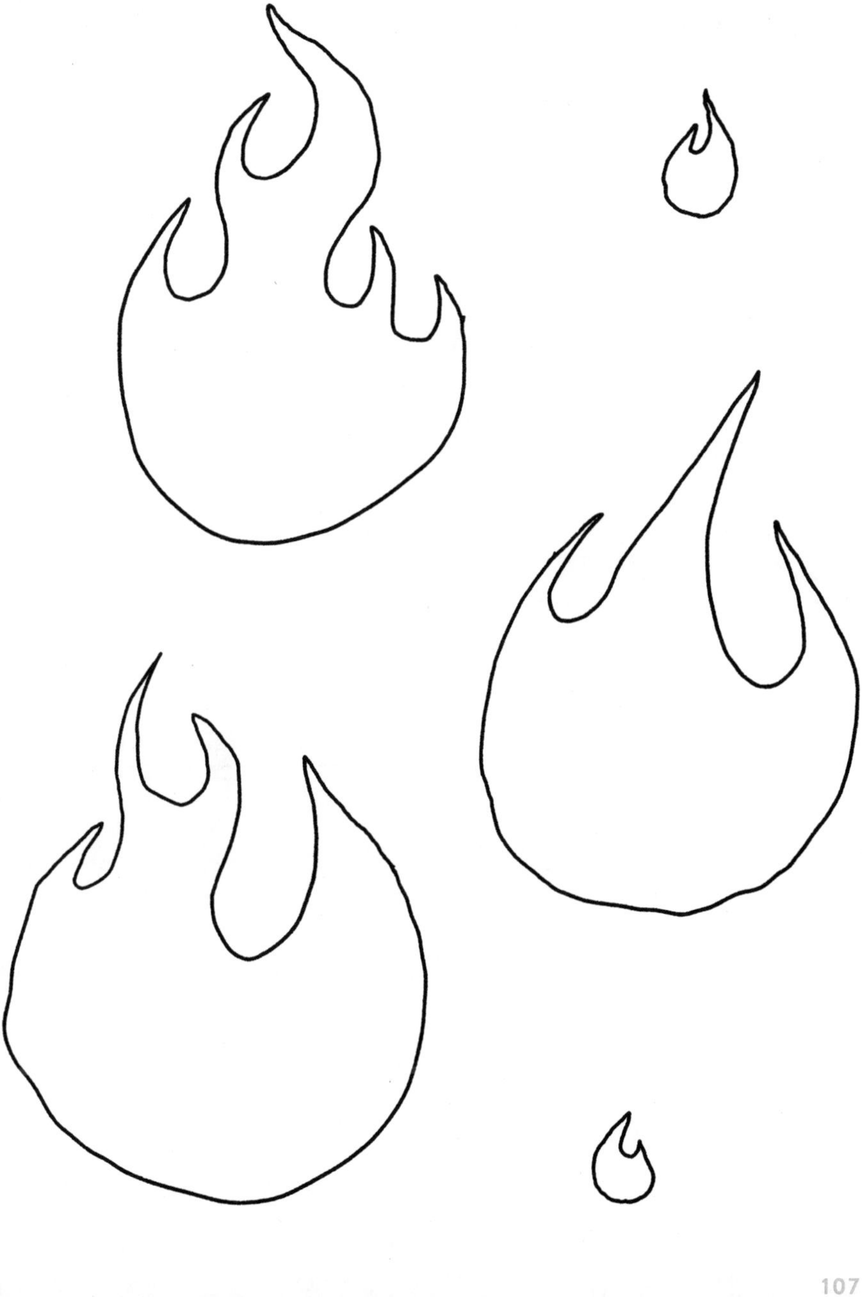

I'D RATHER BE...

Yes, please

IN A PERFECT WORLD...

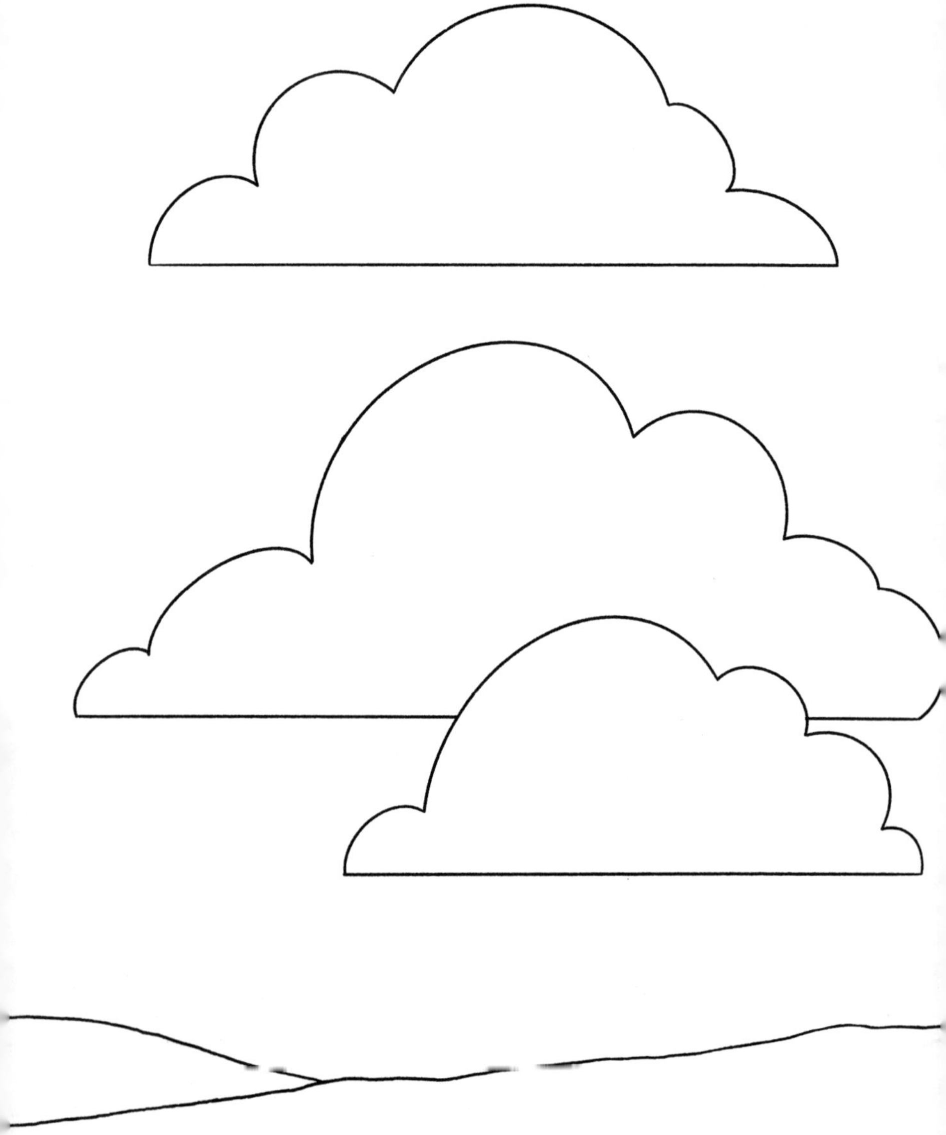

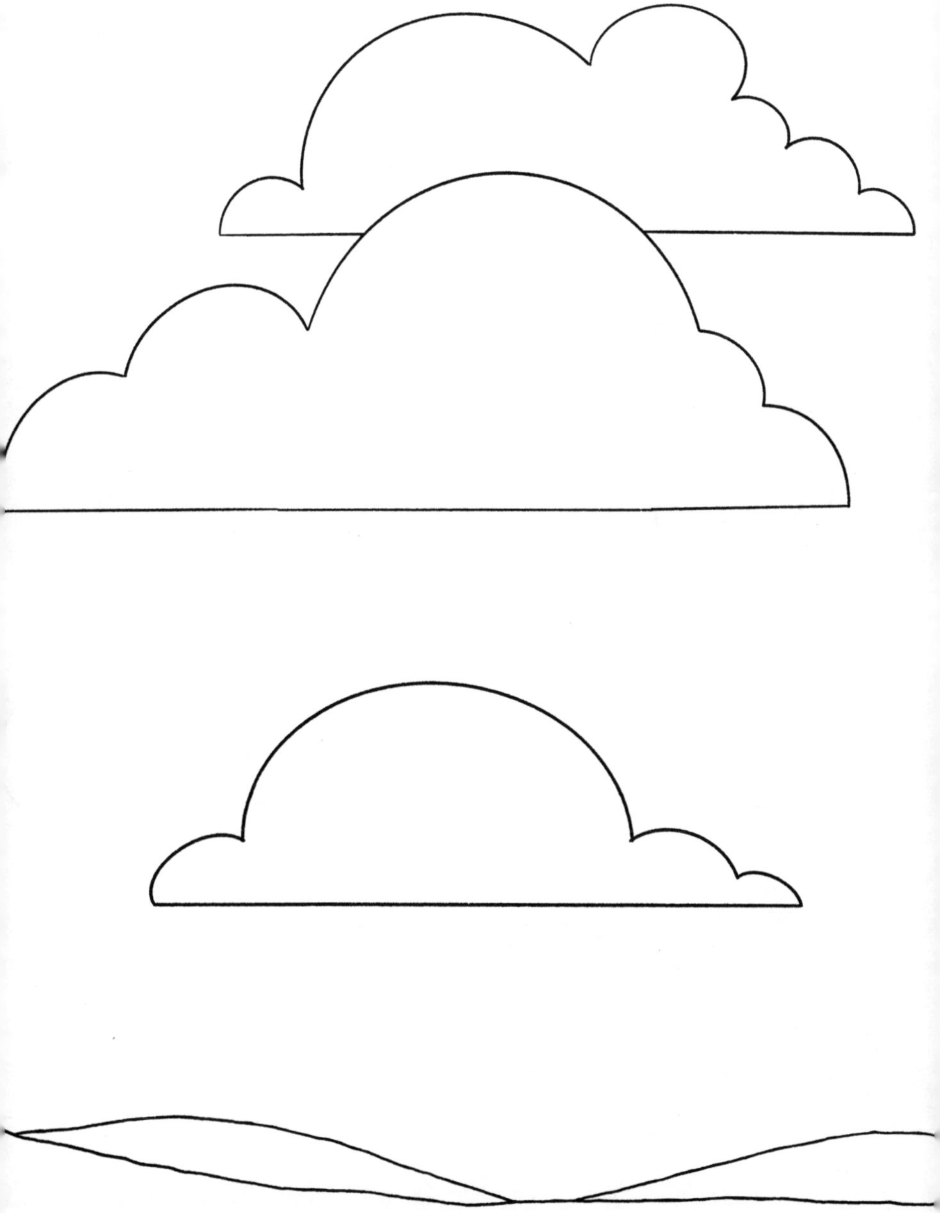

A MESSAGE TO THE HATERS

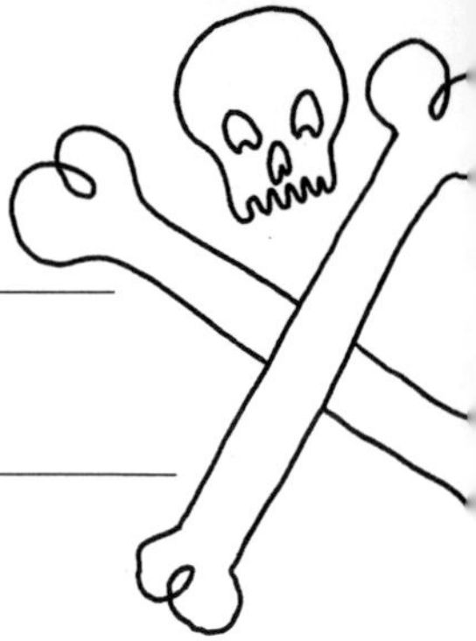

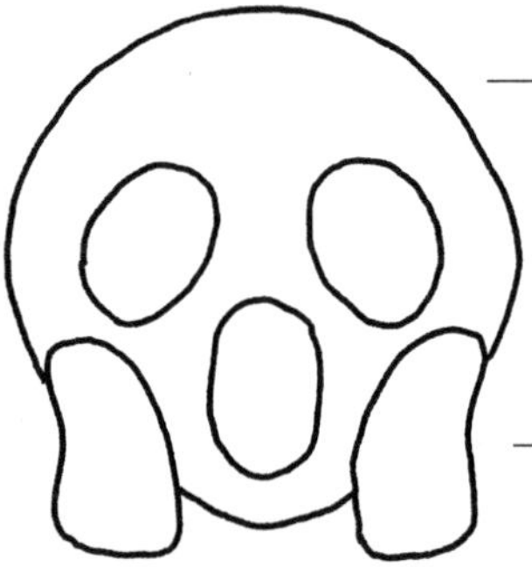

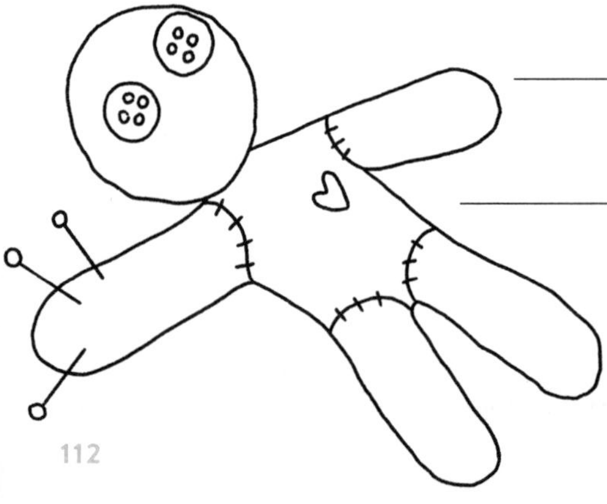

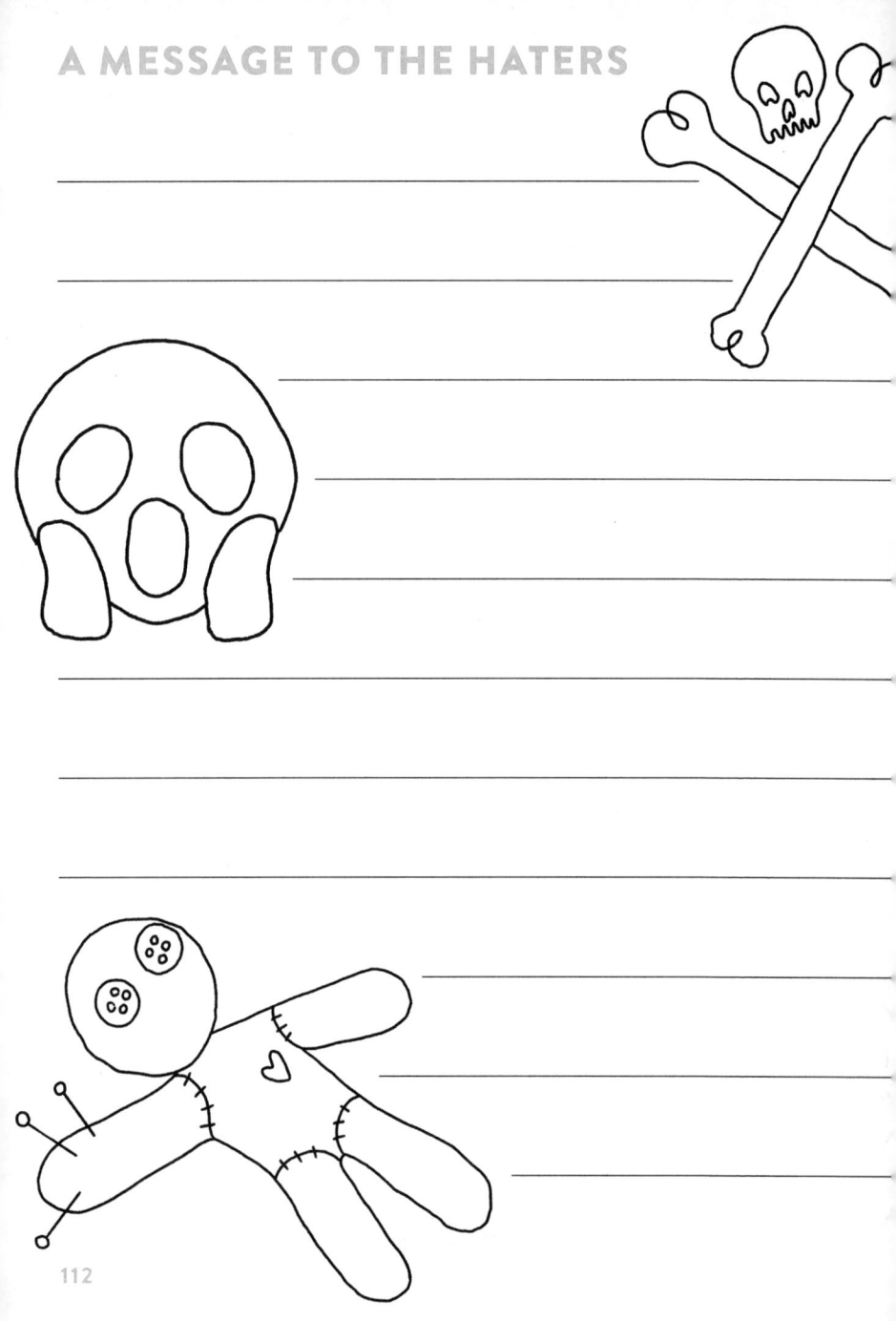

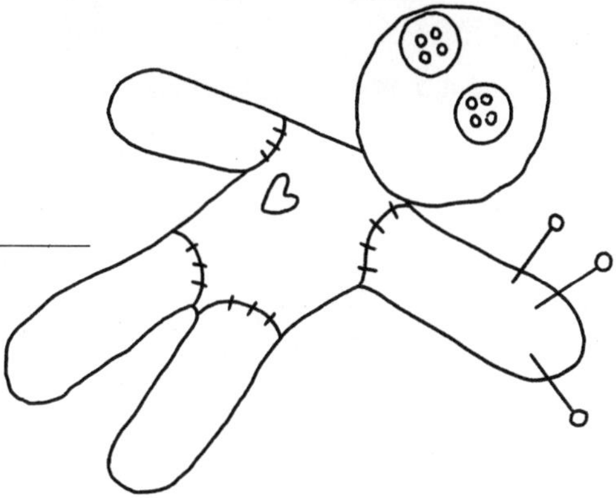

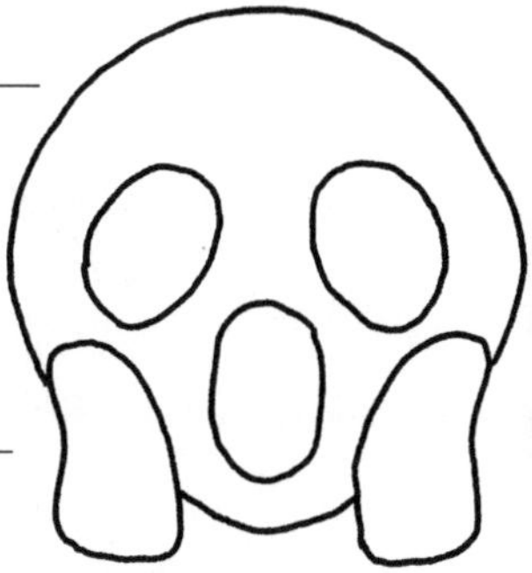

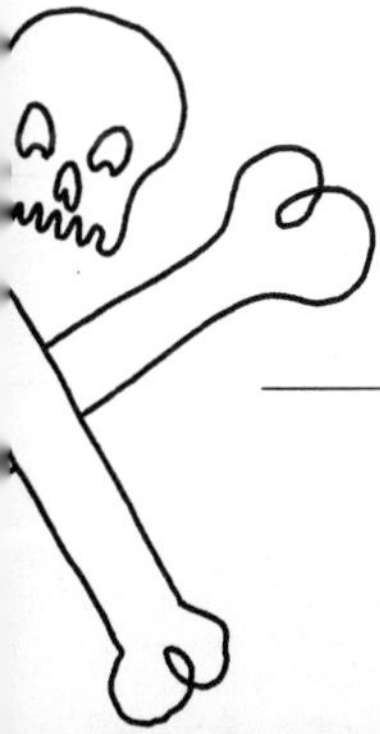

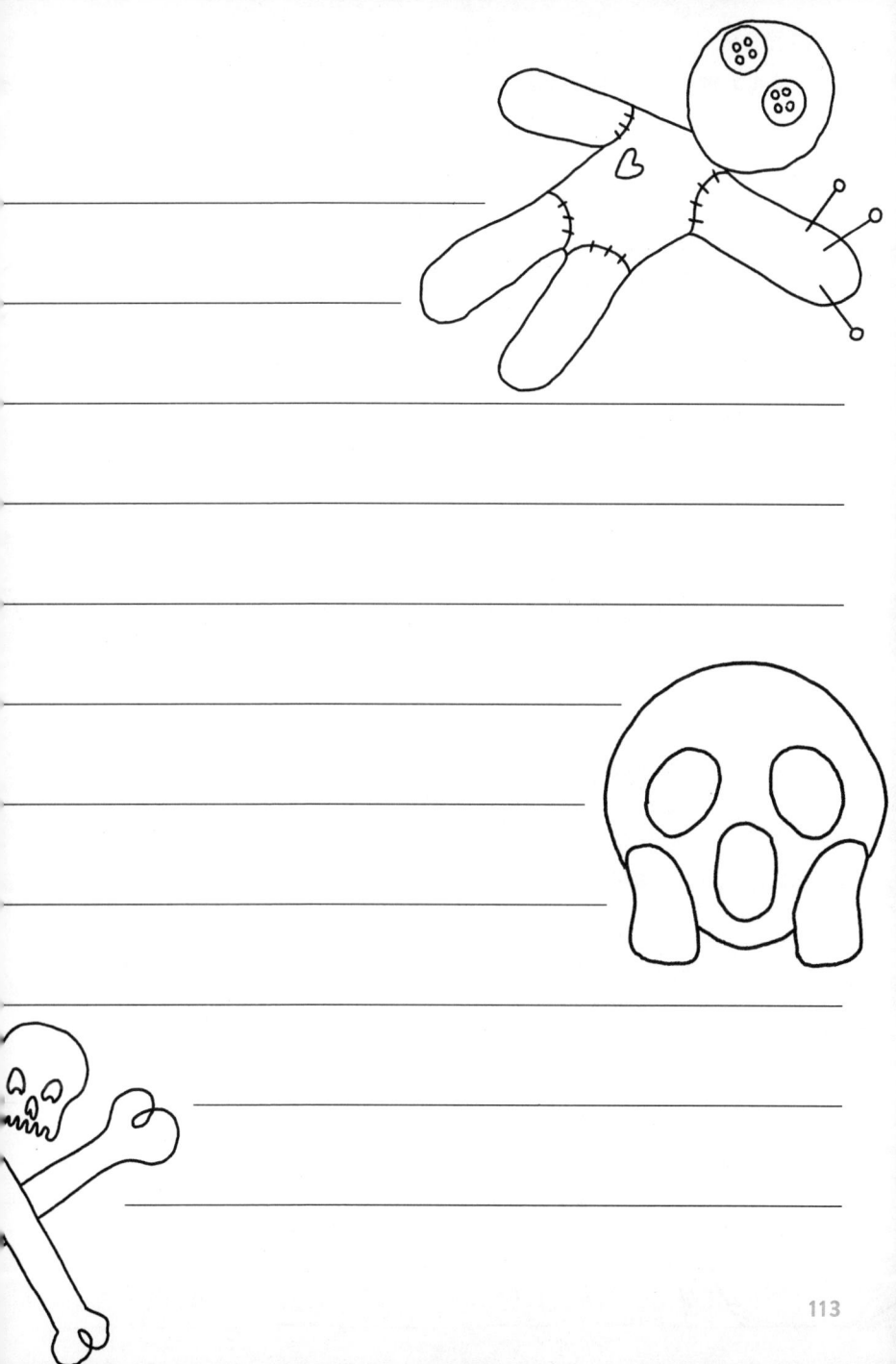

IN MY DREAMS…

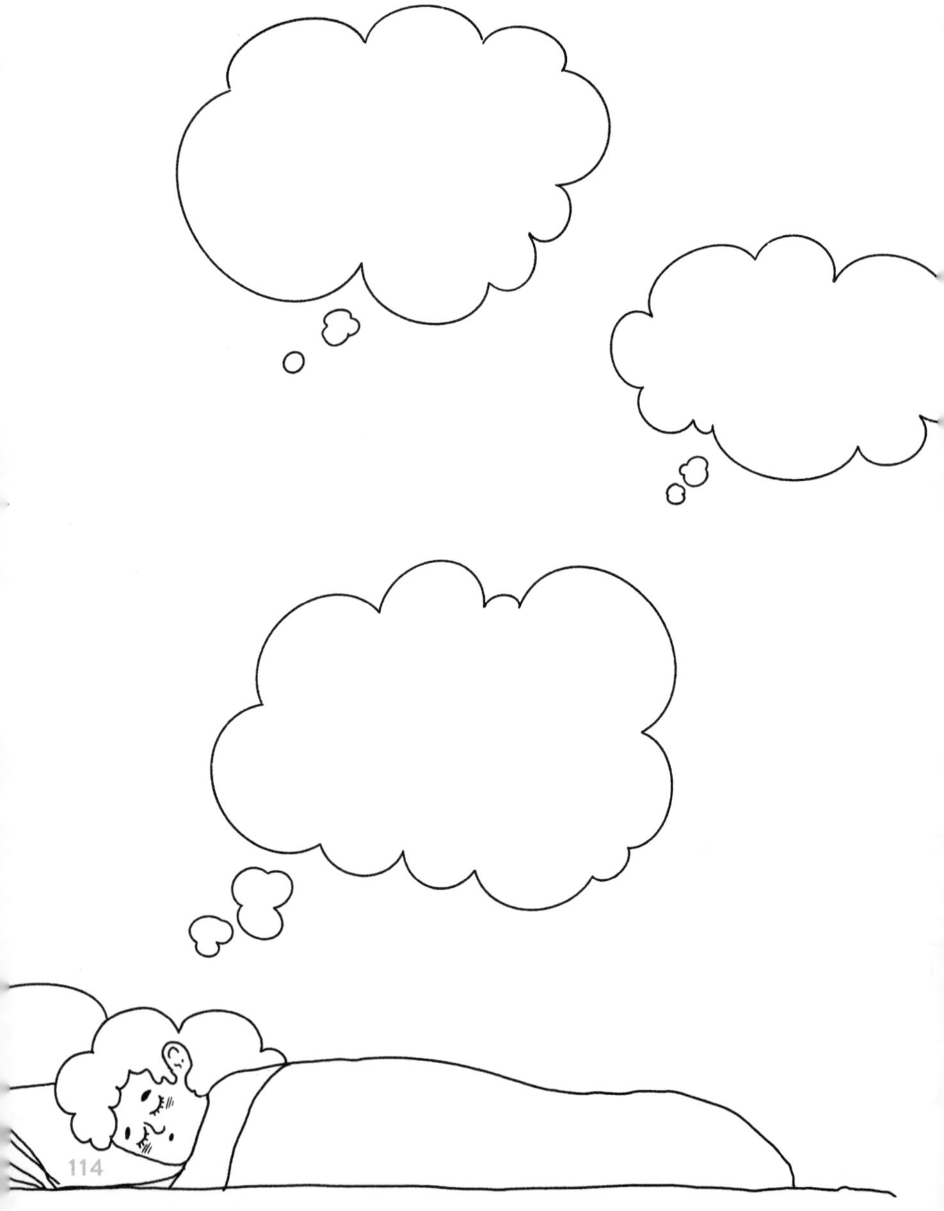

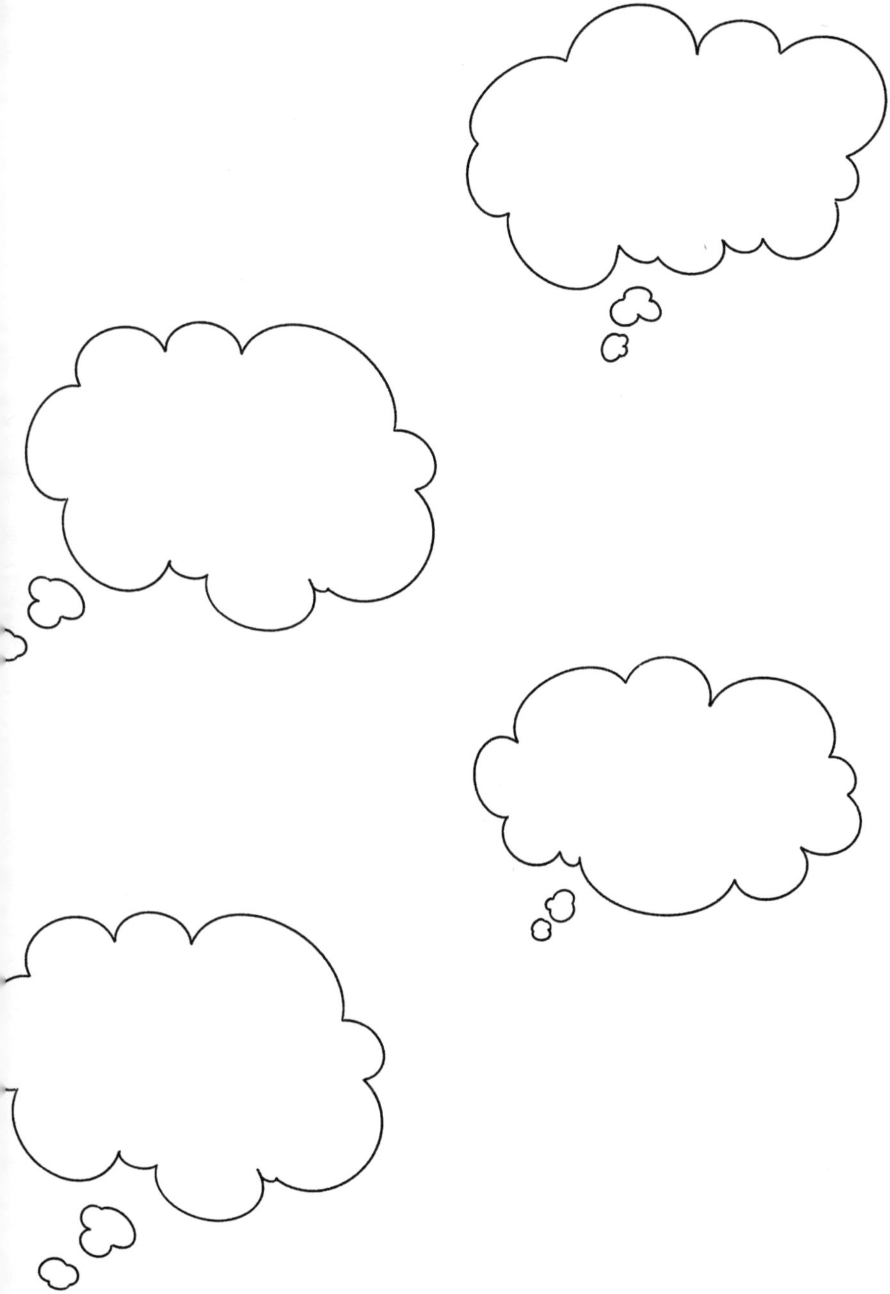

I'M RIGHT ABOUT _____
BECAUSE...

_____

_____

_____

_____

_____

_____

_____

_____

_____

_____

_____

CAN'T GET ENOUGH...

More,
more,
more

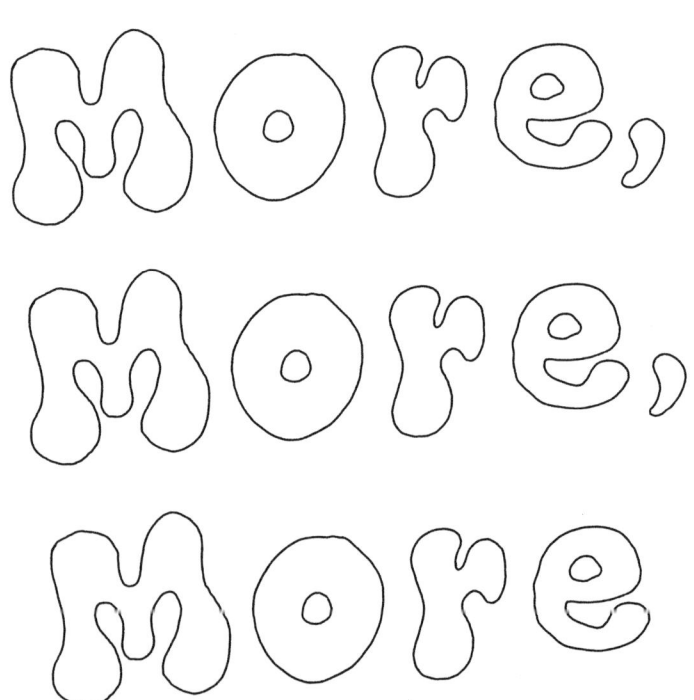

TOTALLY OVER...

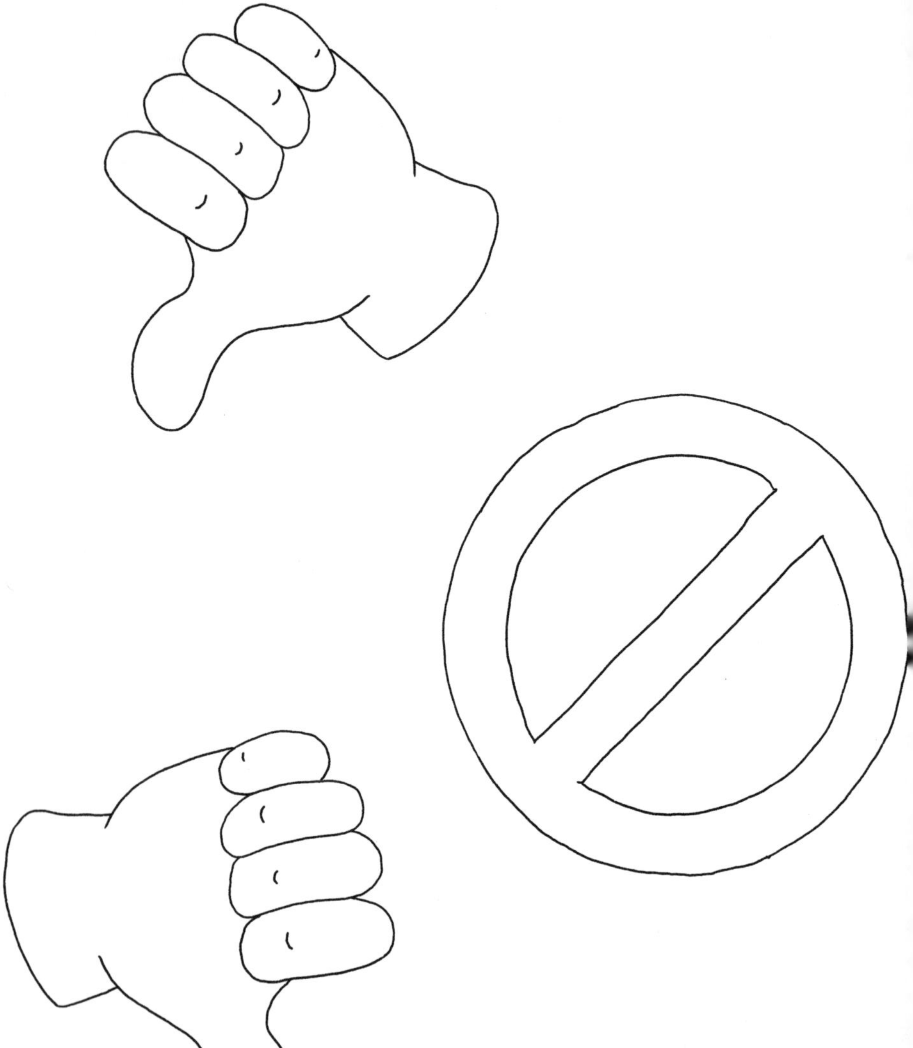

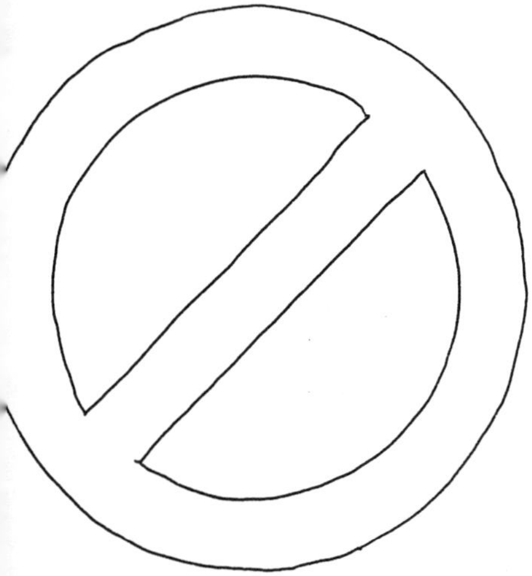

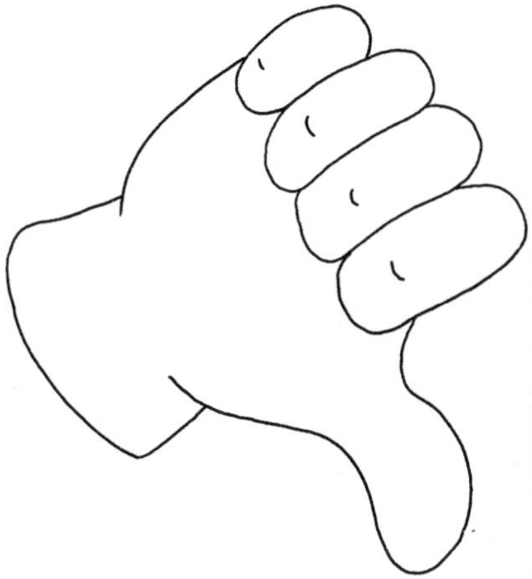

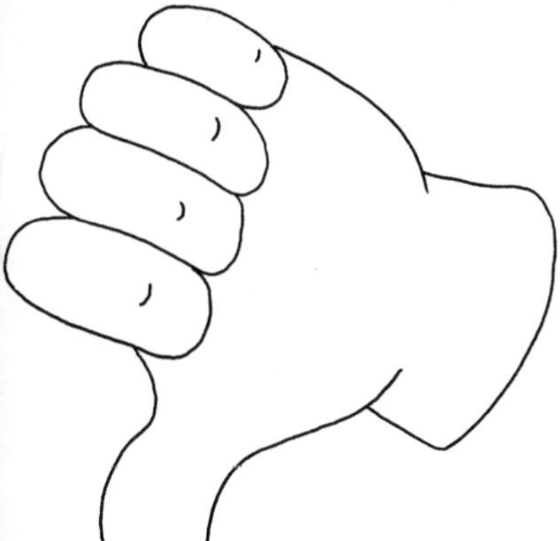

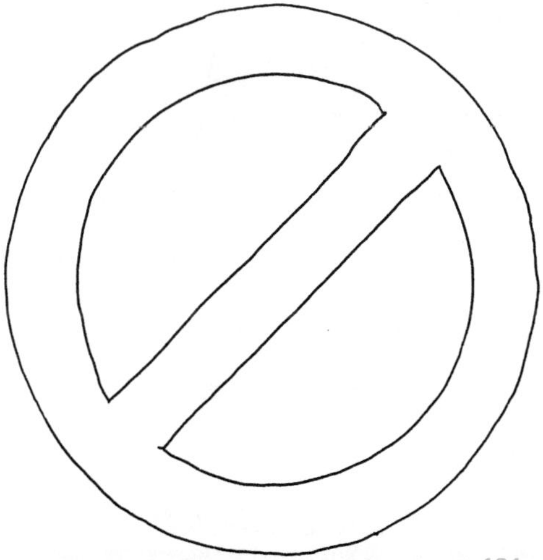

THIRSTY FOR...

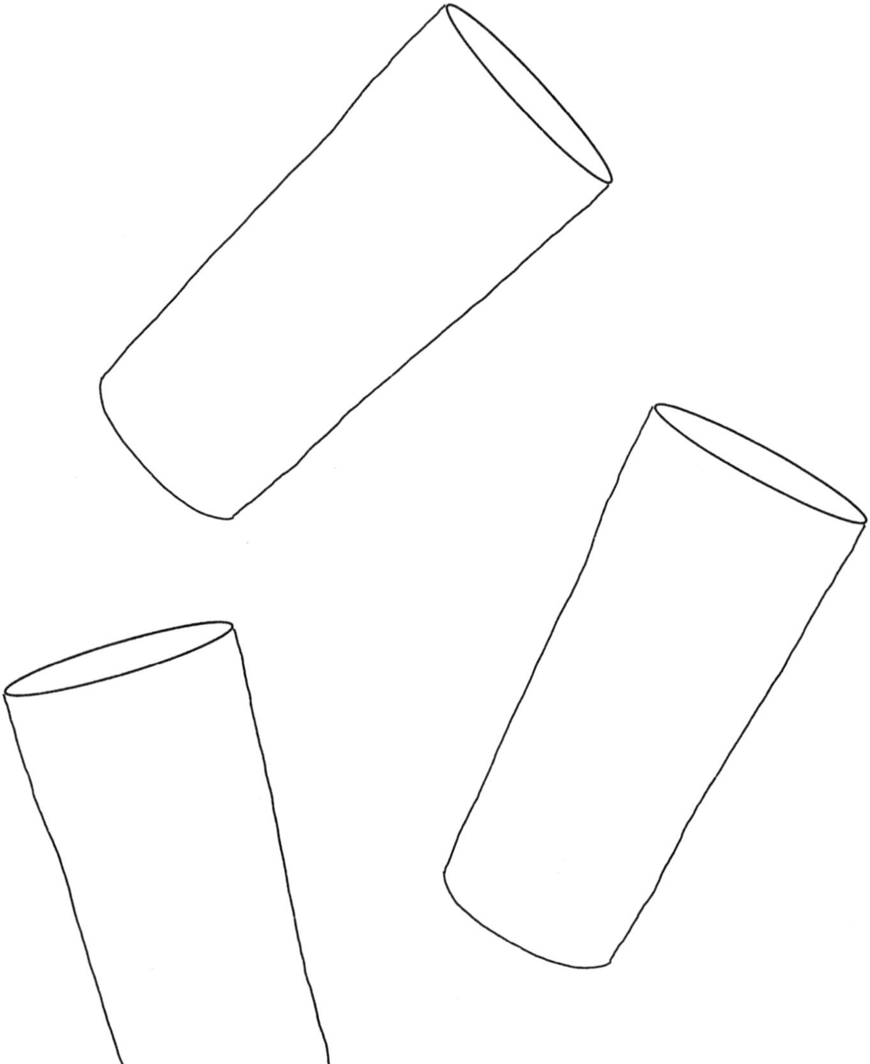

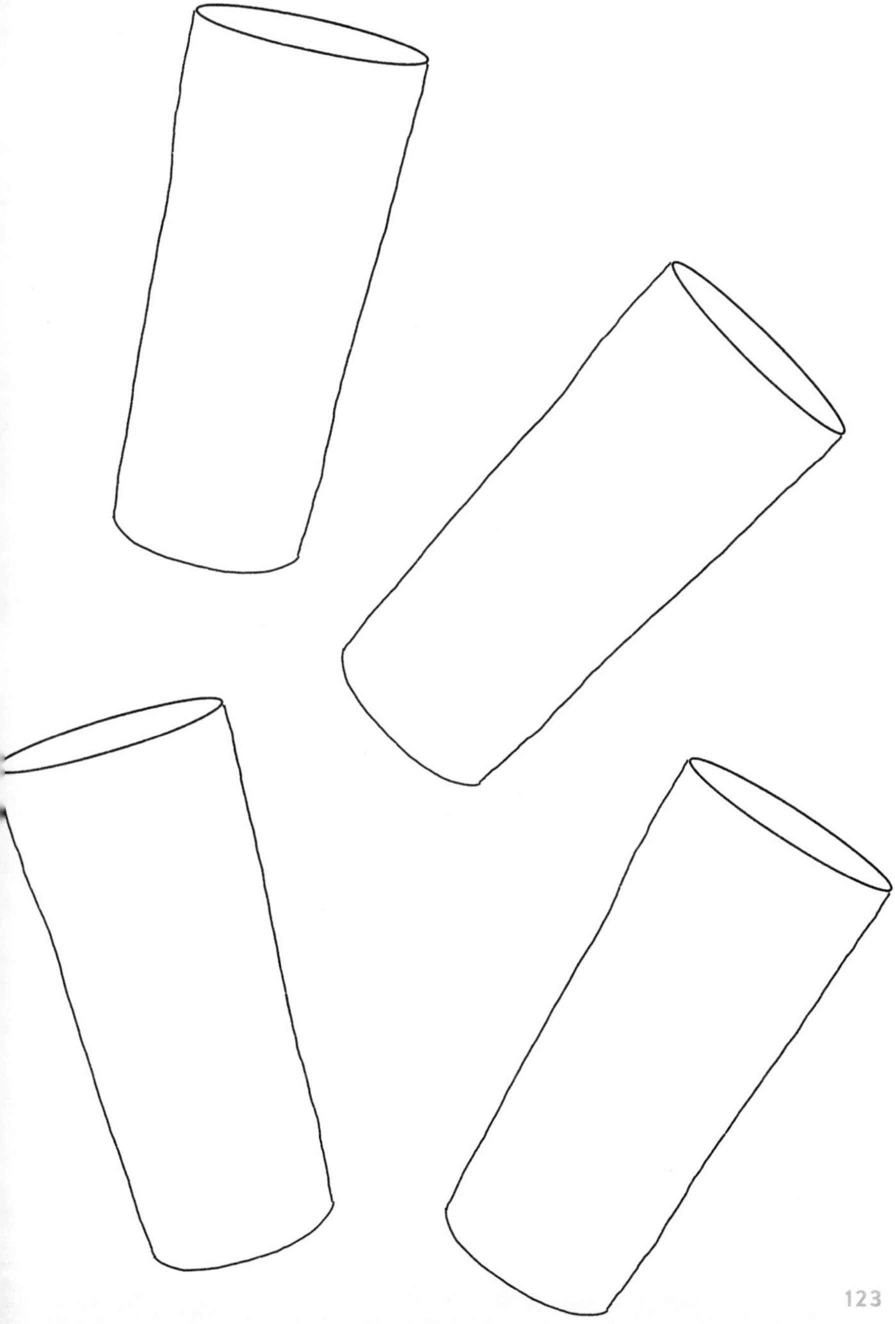

MUST-HAVES

$$\bigcirc\!\!\!\!\!\!\!\diagdown \text{substitutes}$$

THIS DESERVES A MEDAL

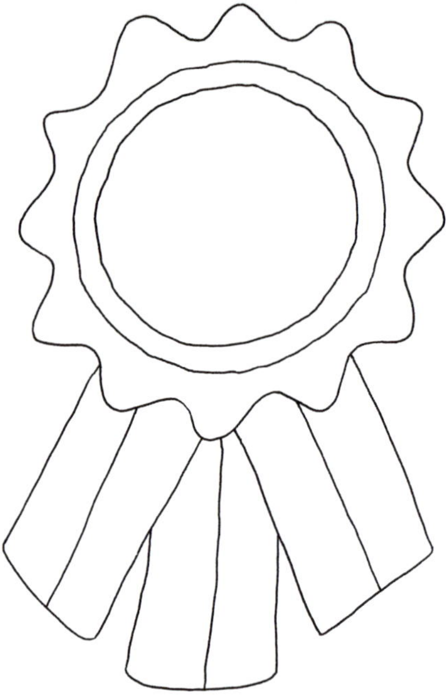

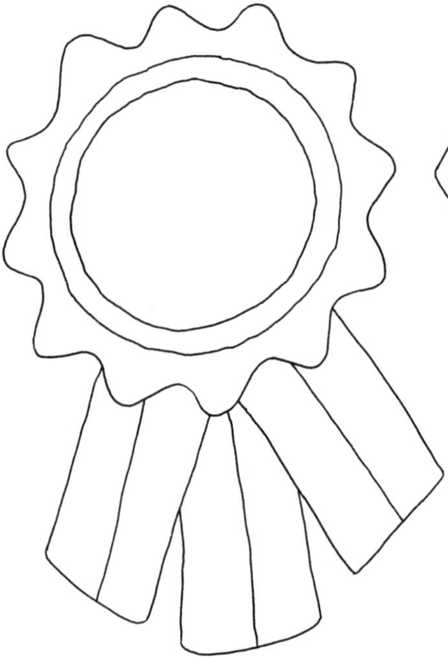

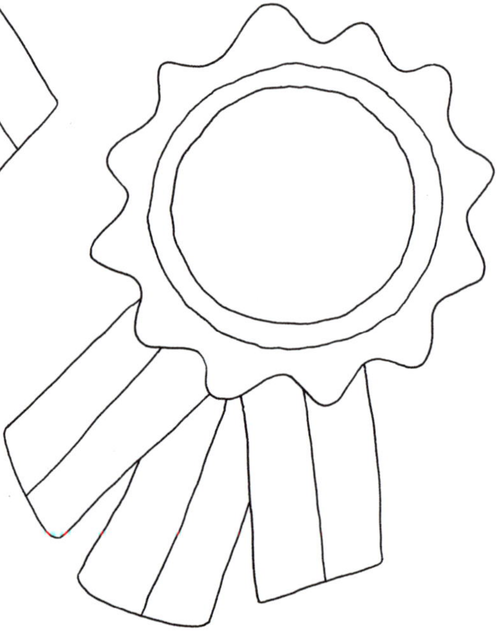

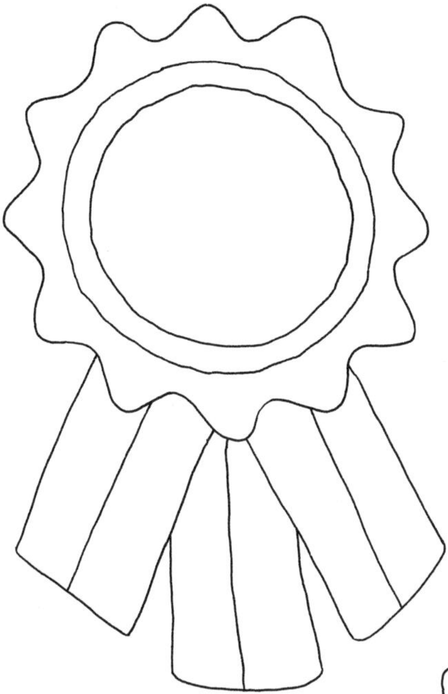

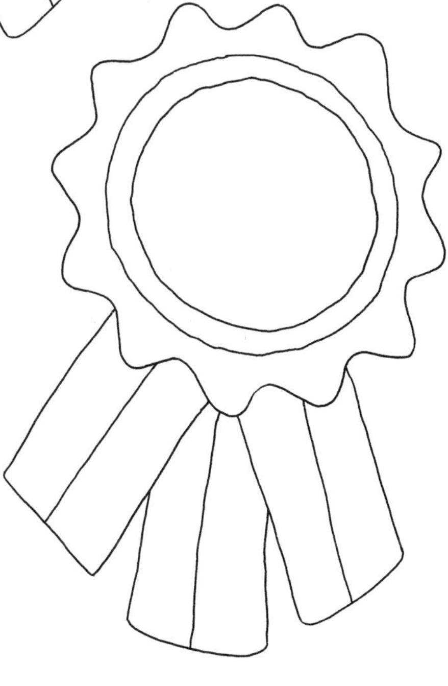

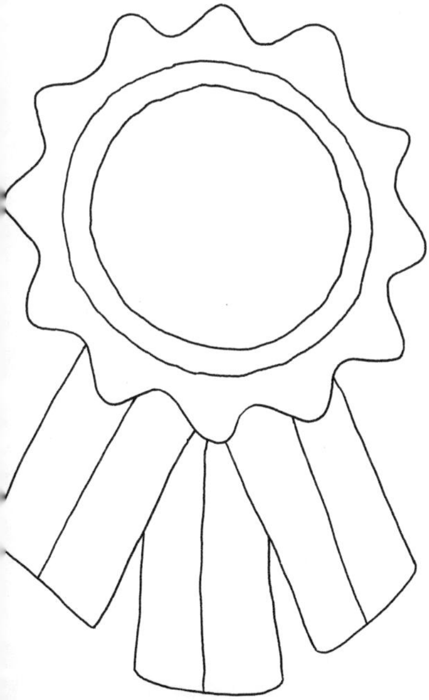

#OOTD

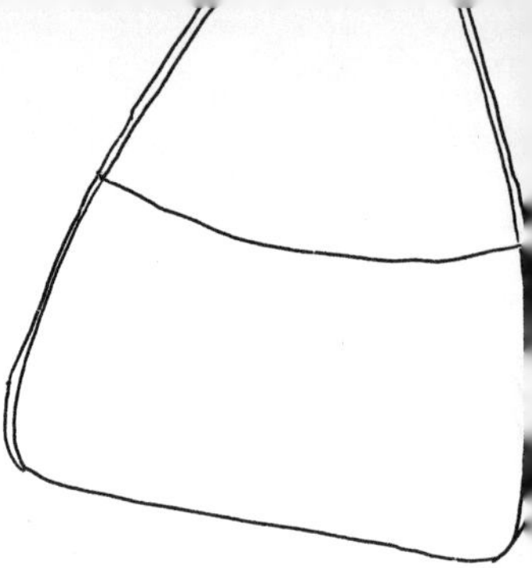

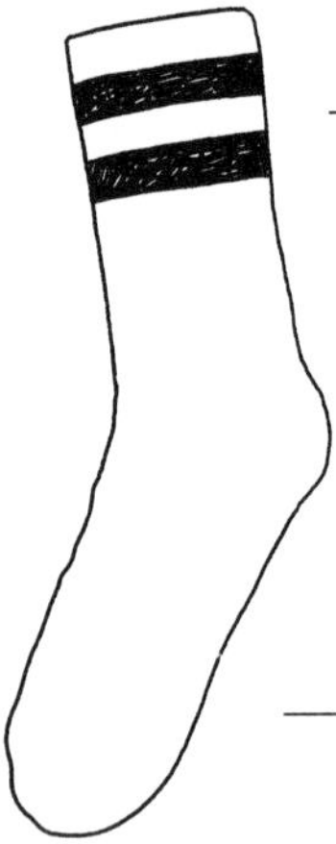

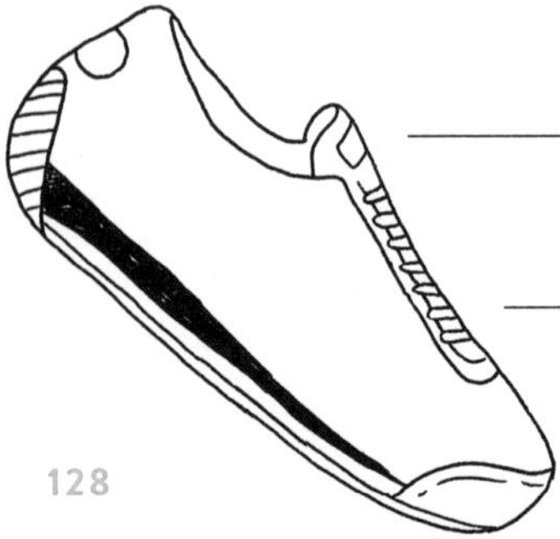

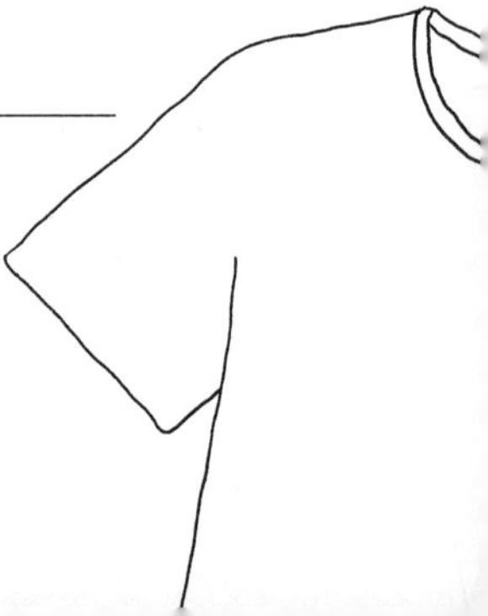

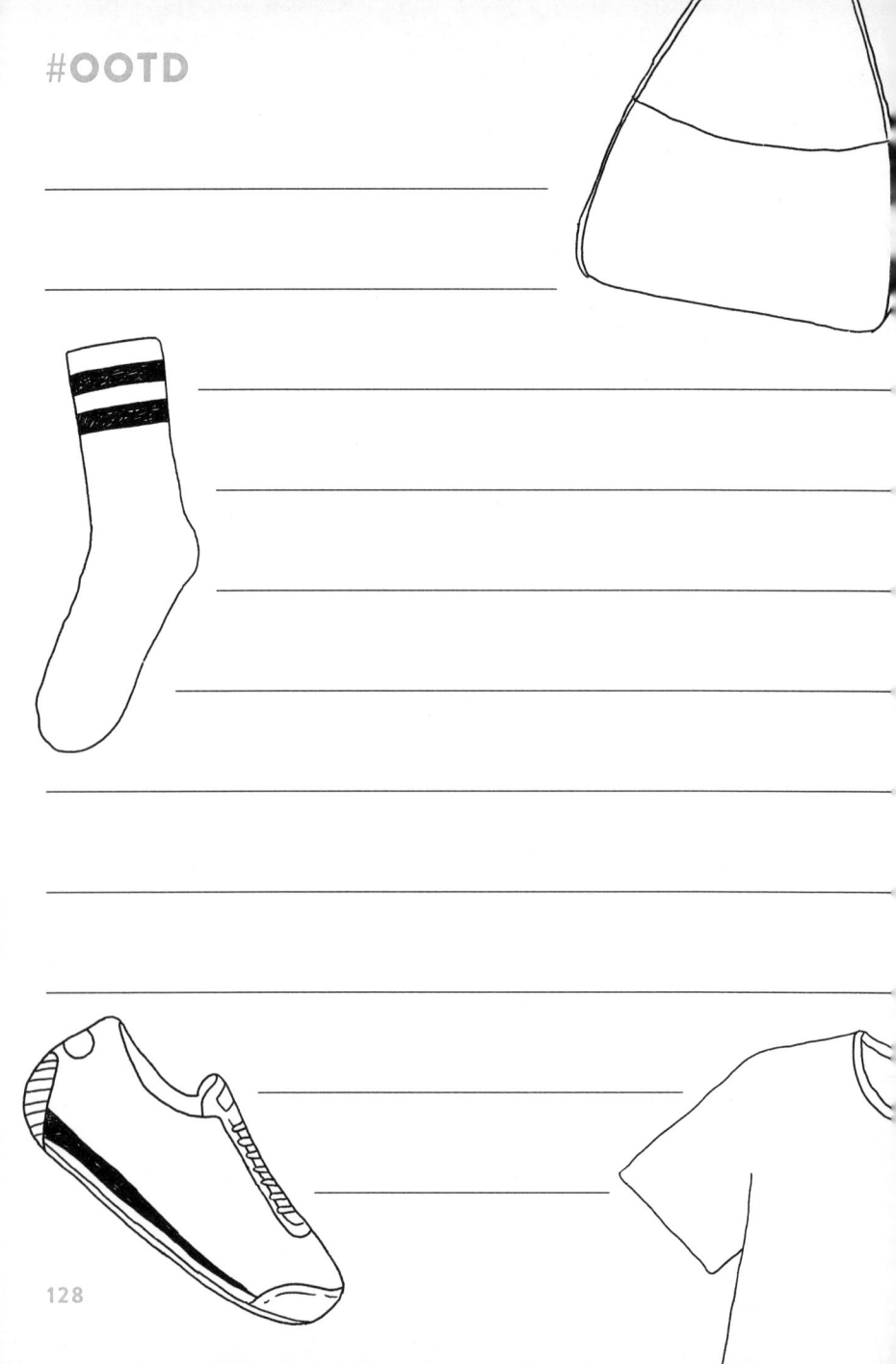

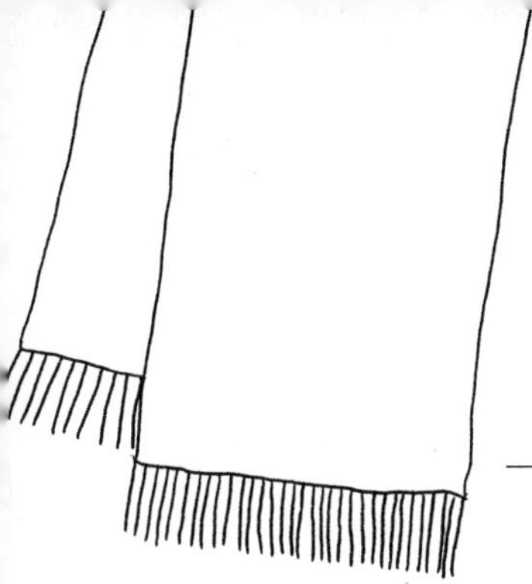
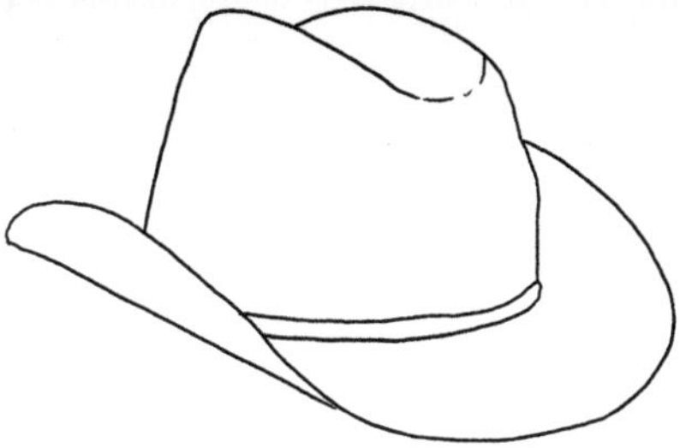
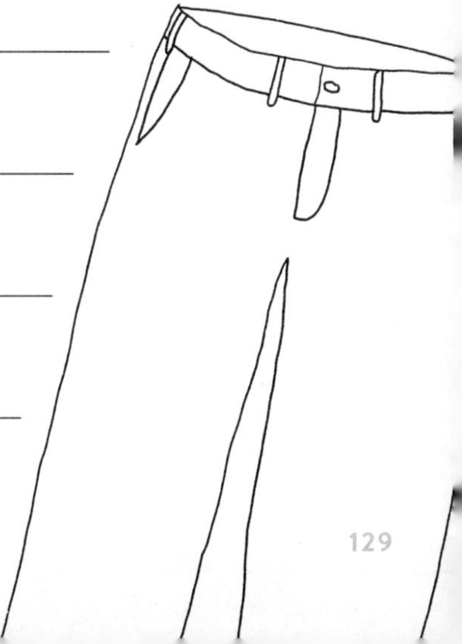
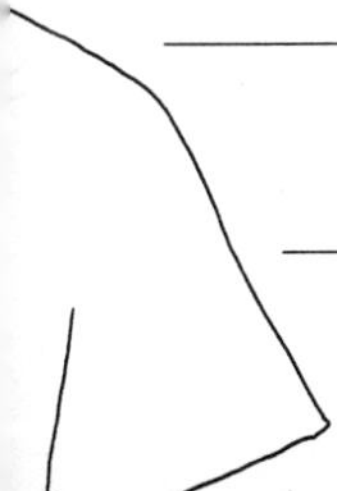

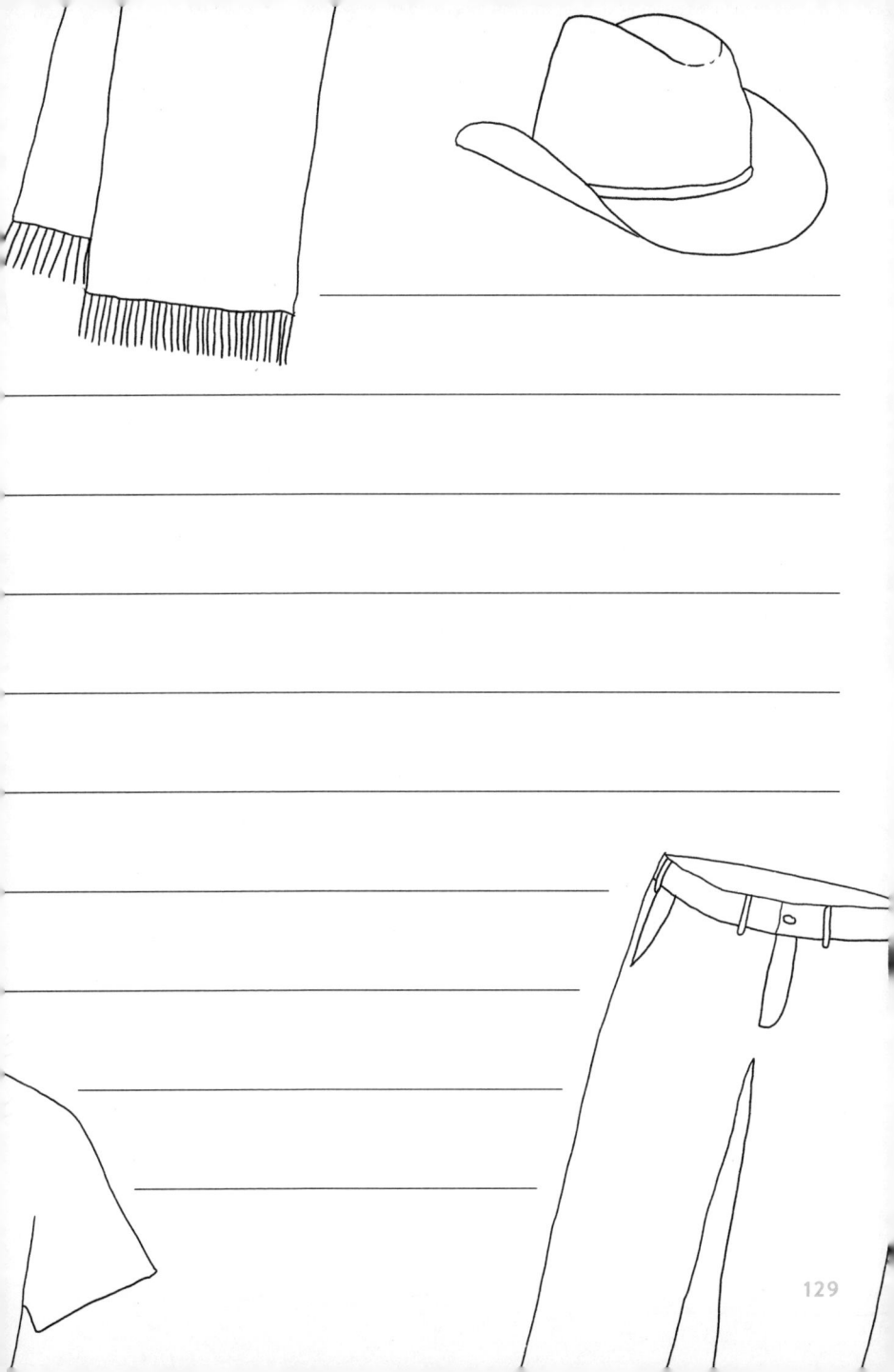

MY DESERT ISLAND PACKING LIST

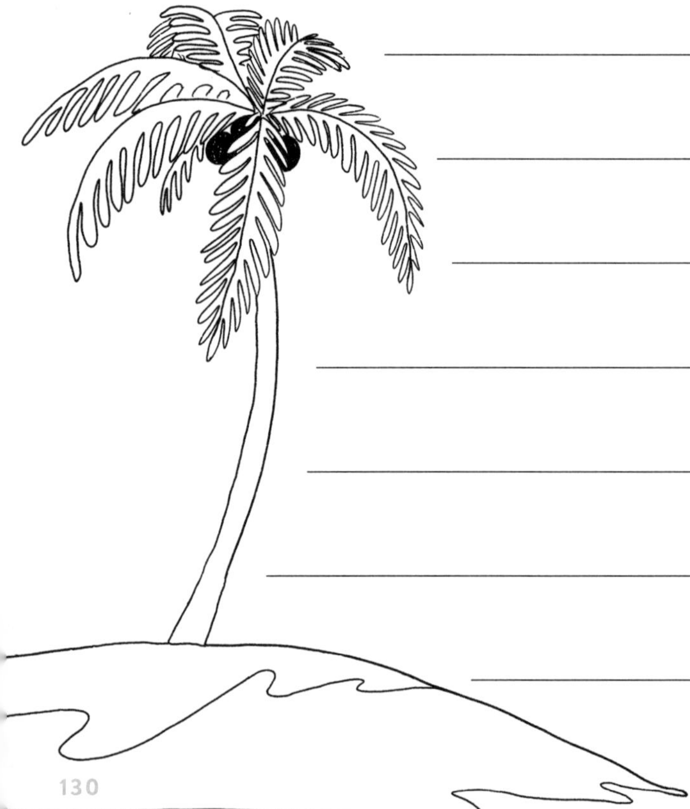

WHY HAVEN'T WE...?

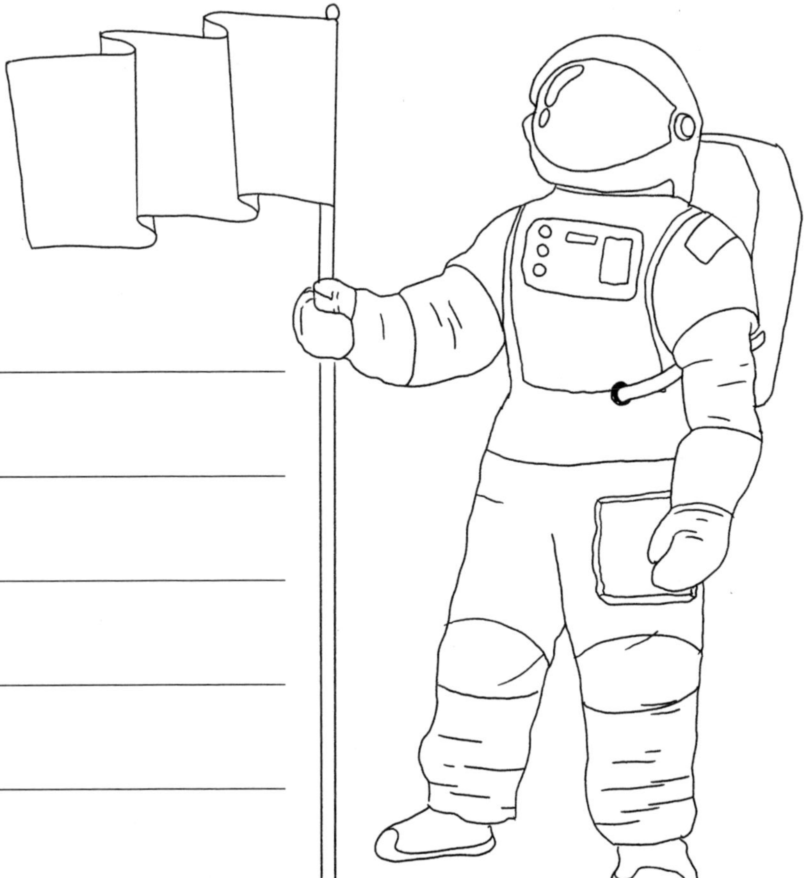

SUPER CRINGEY

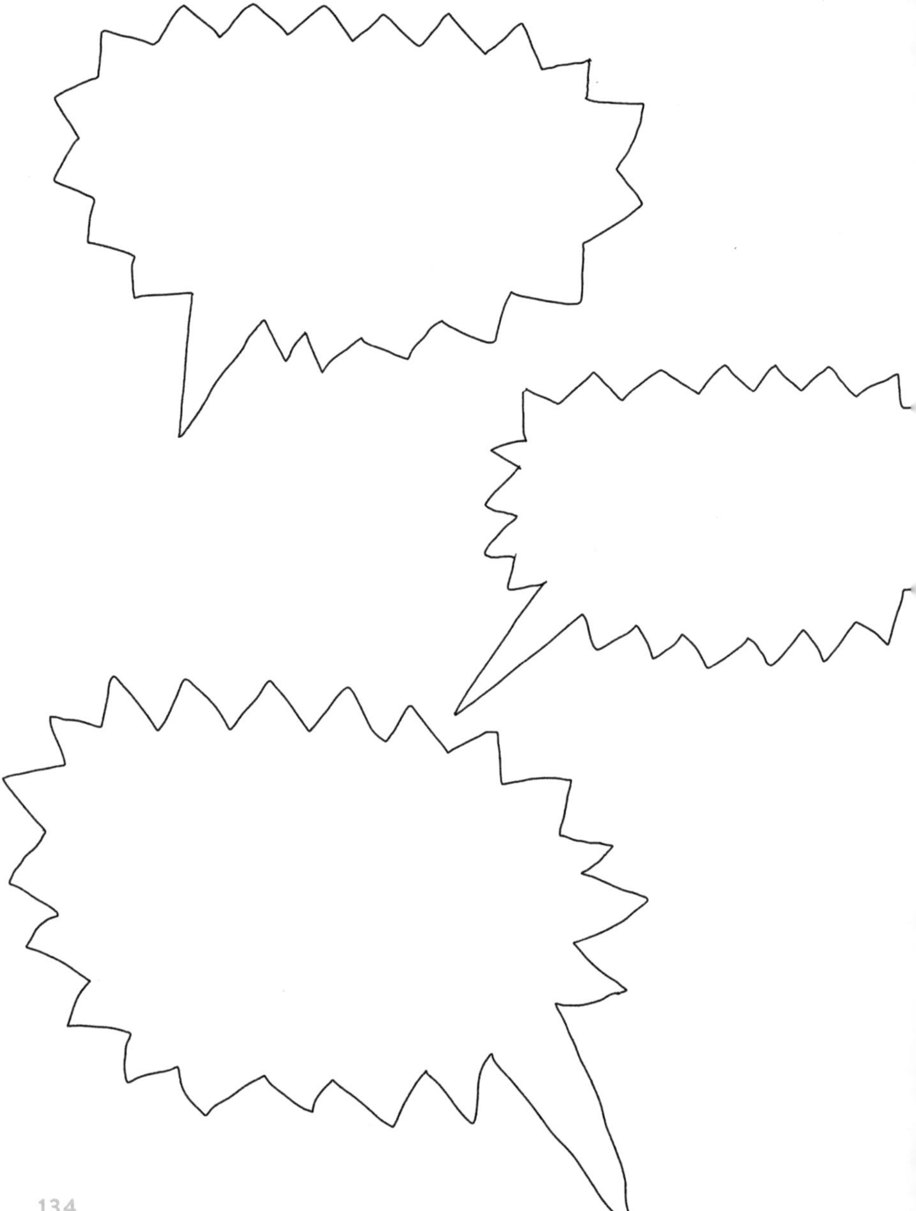

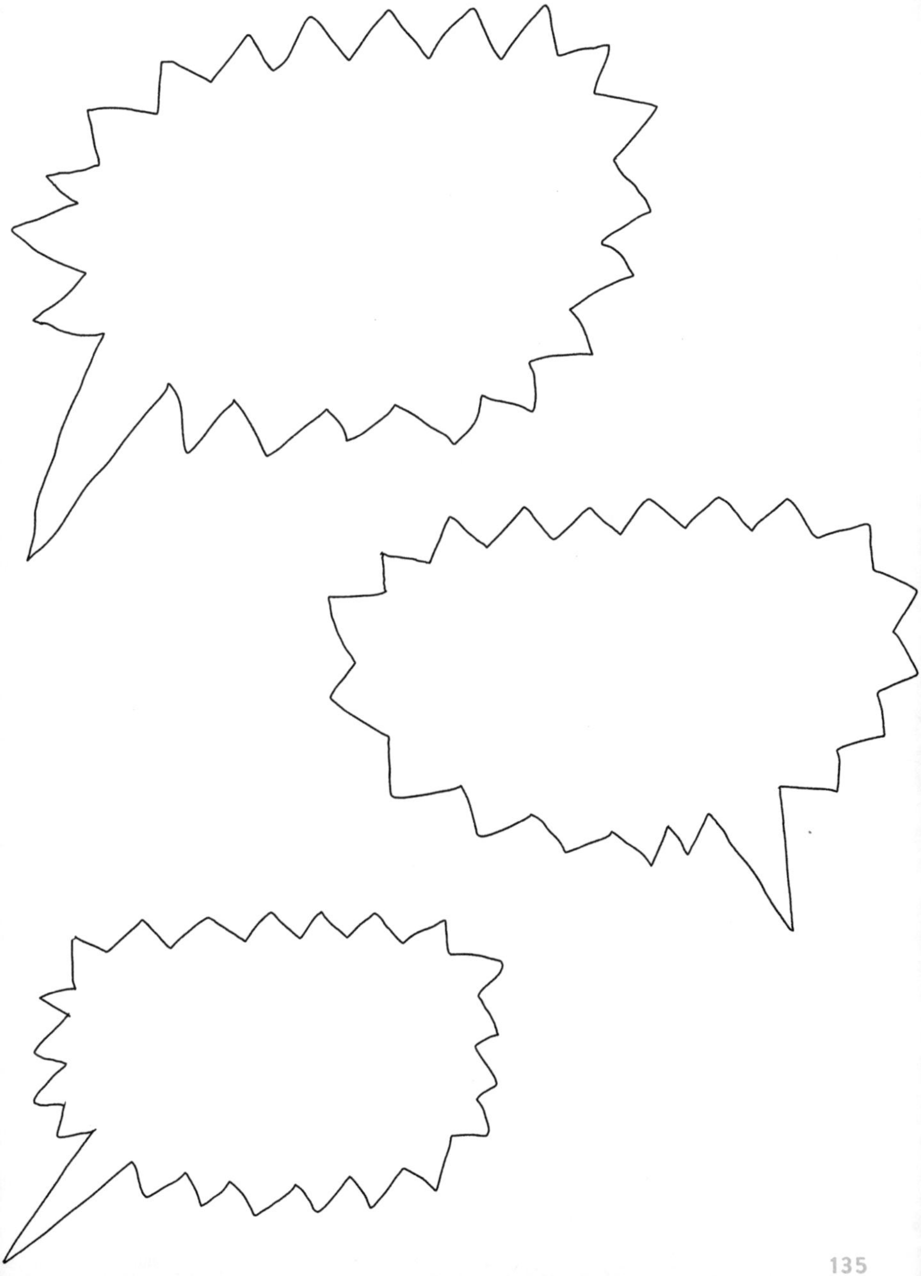

HEROES

VILLAINS

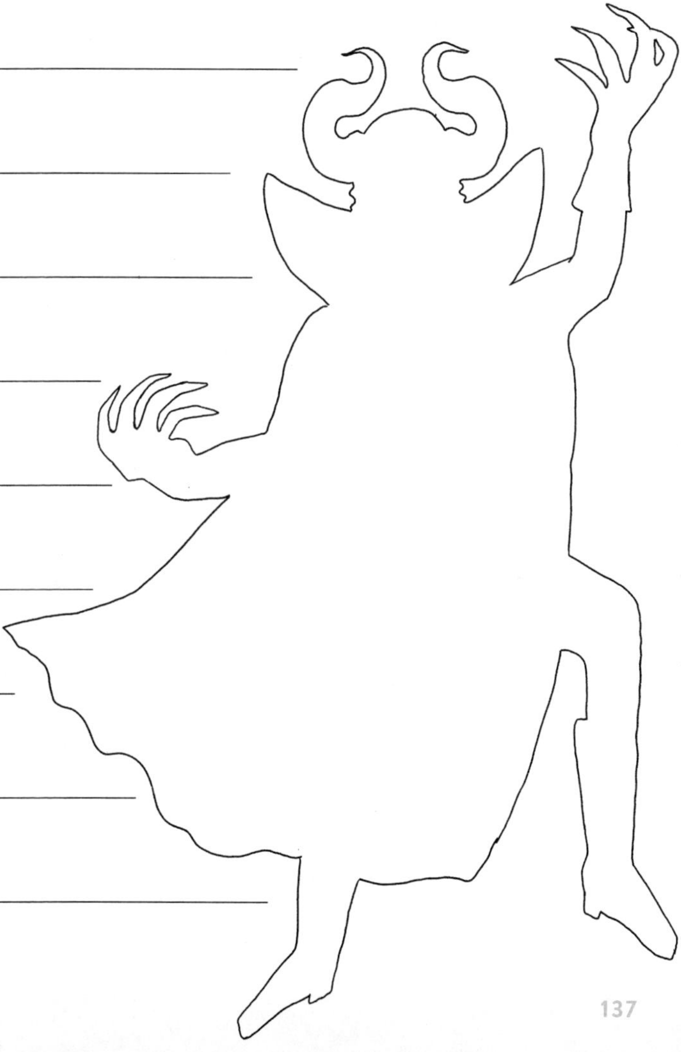

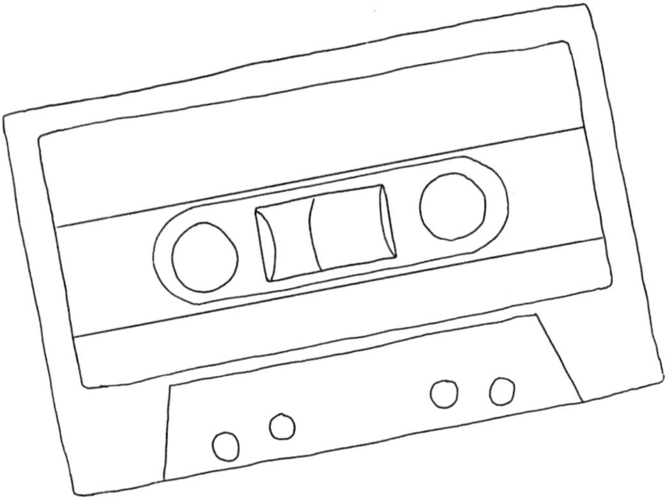

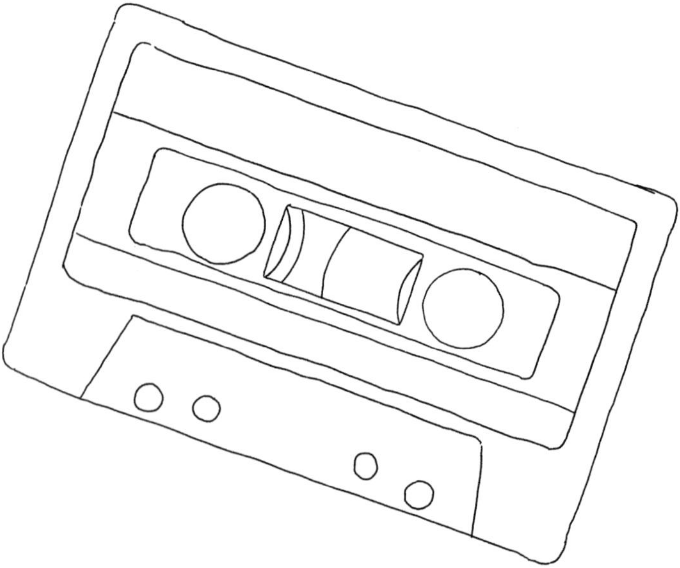

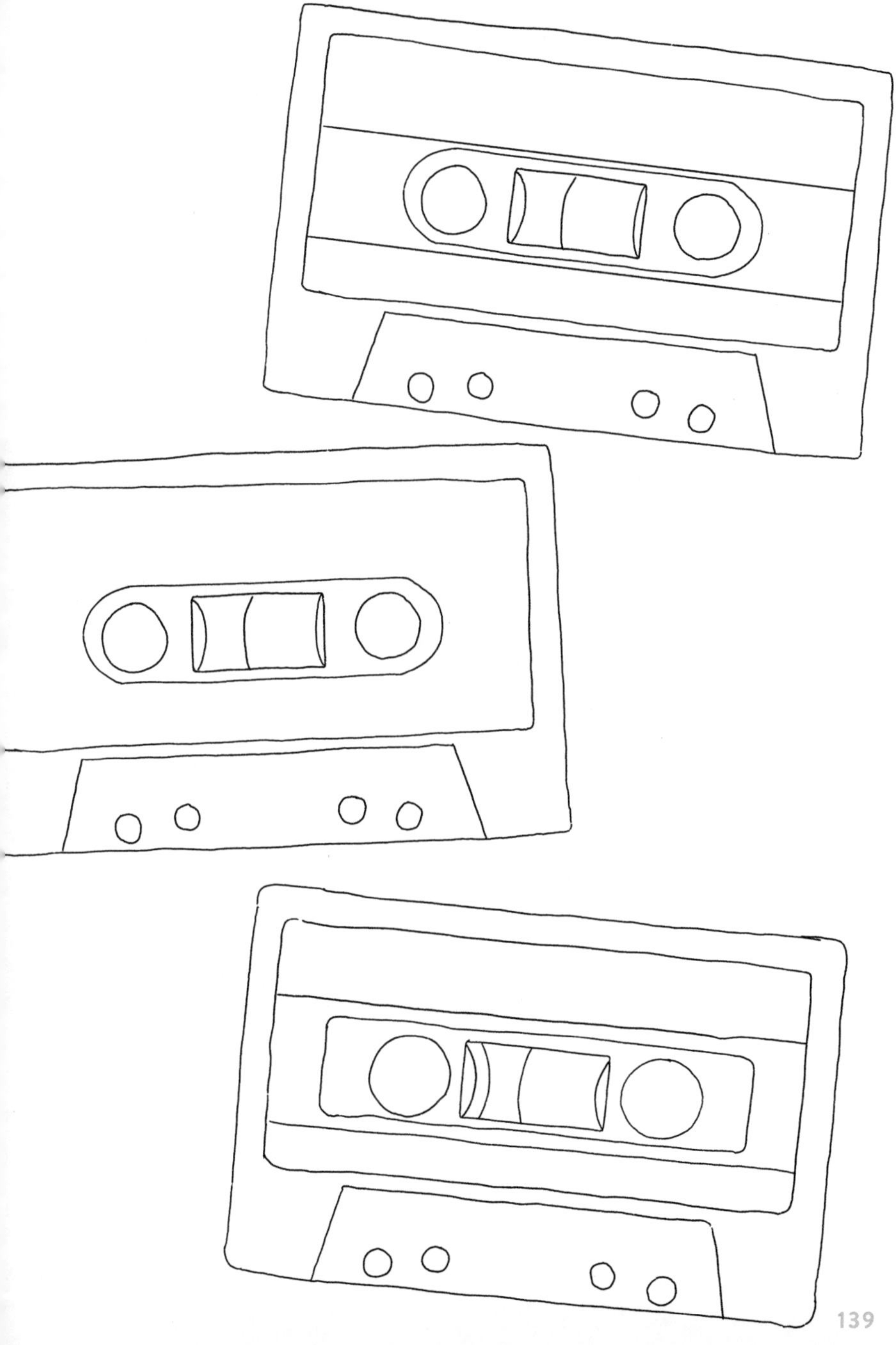

WHAT'S COOKING?

_____

_____

_____

_____

_____

THAT WAS AWKWARD

BEST SMELLS IN THE WORLD

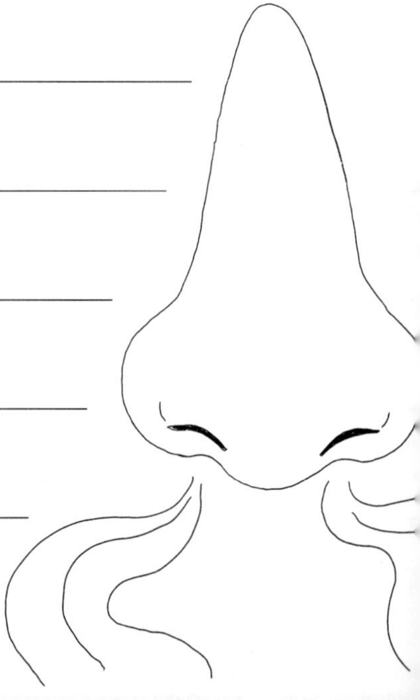

TOTALLY LIT

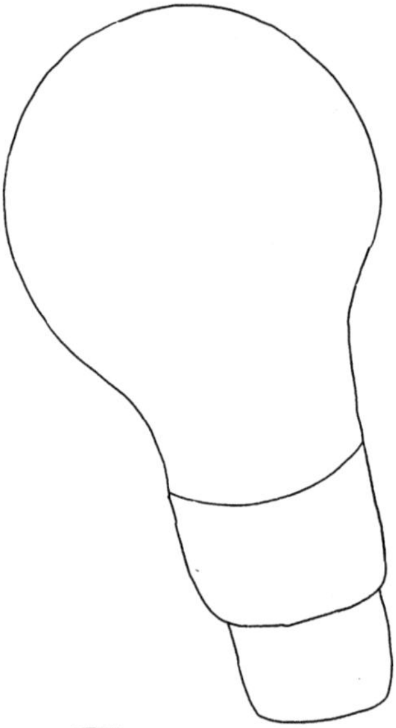

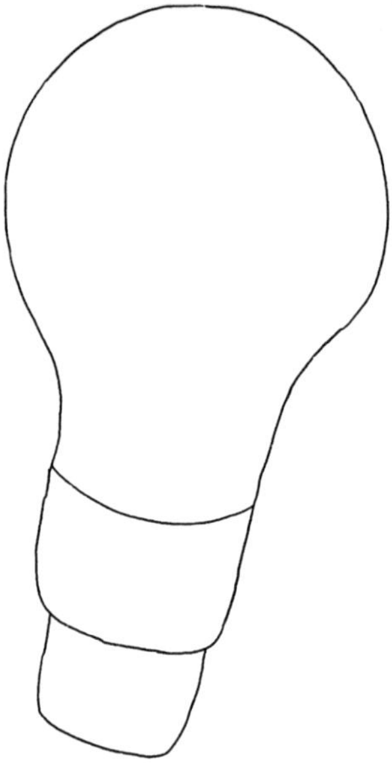

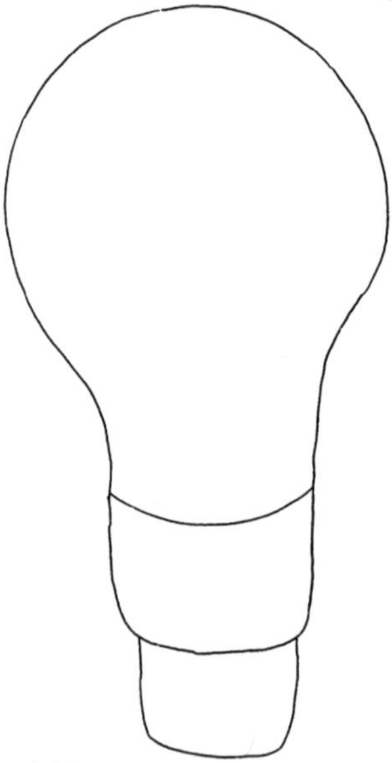

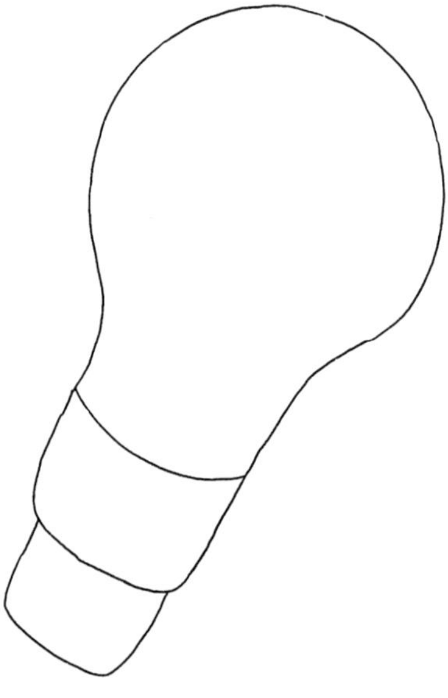

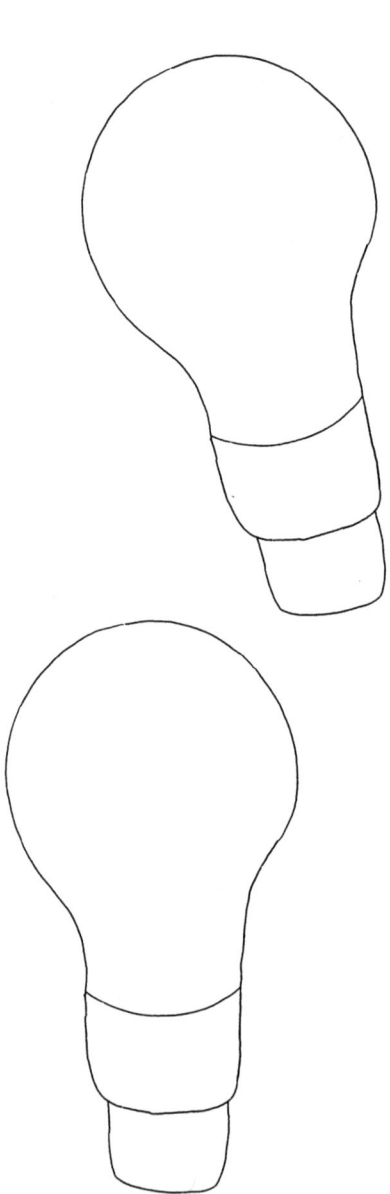

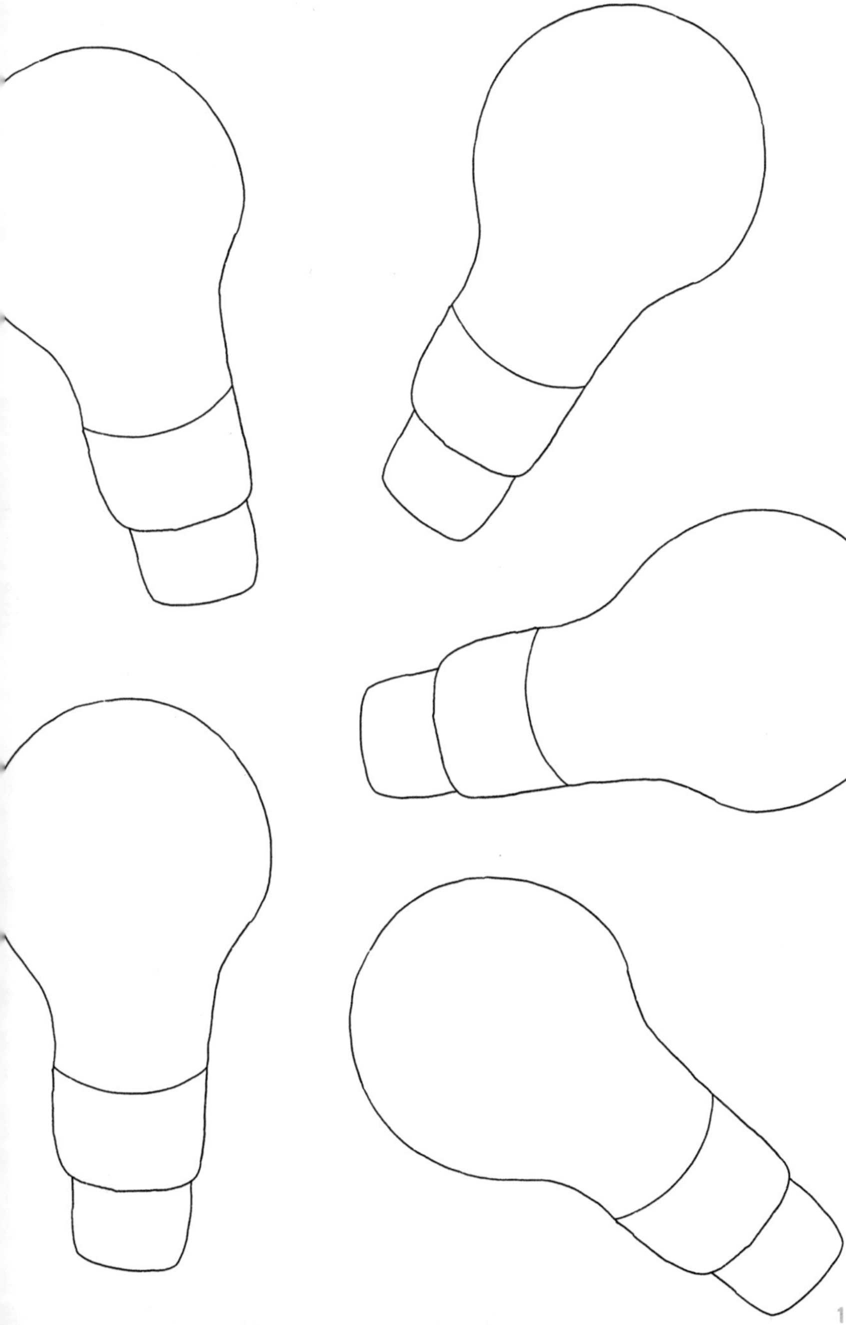

CAN YOU BELIEVE THIS?

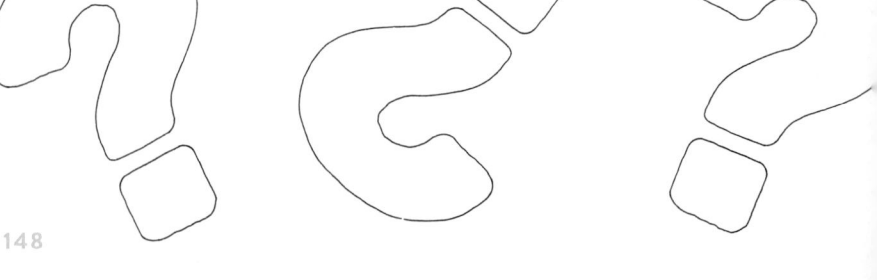

#TOBEREAD

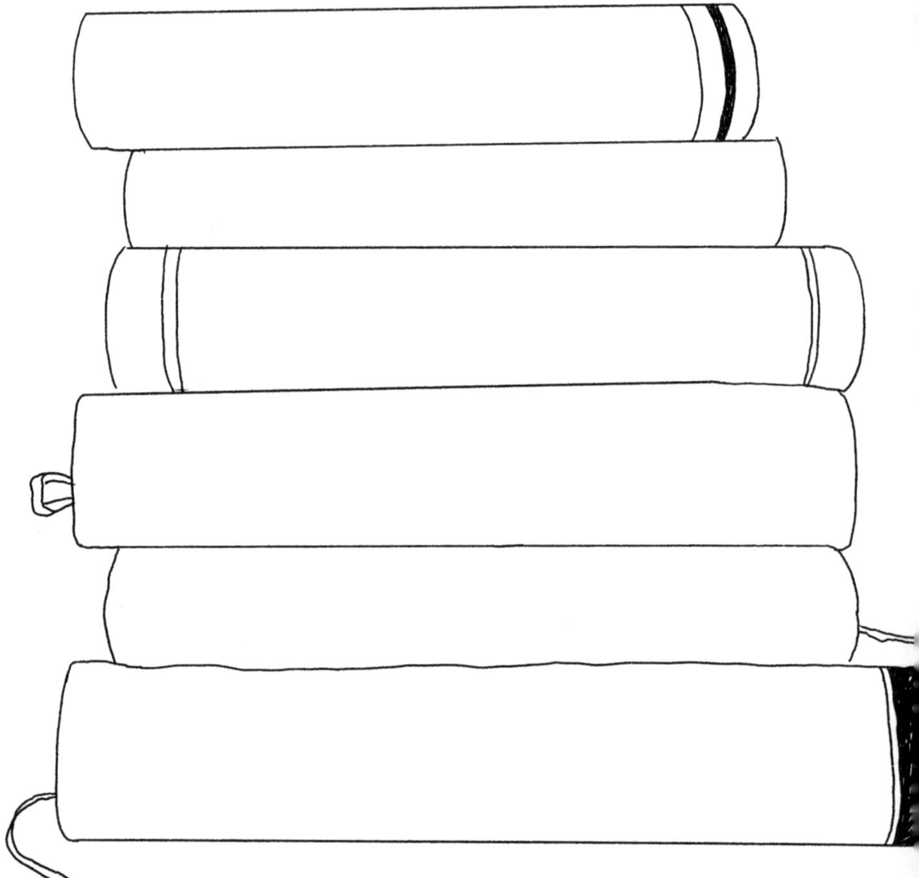

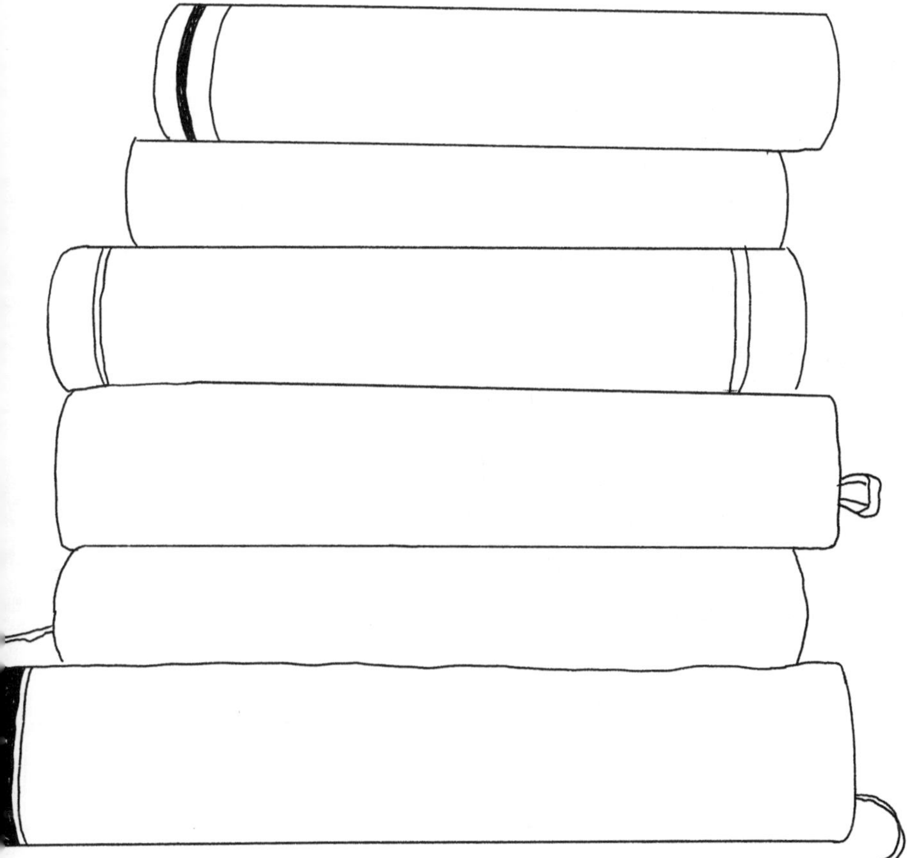

UNPOPULAR OPINION

I'M JUST SAYIN'

THE BEST THINGS OF THIS YEAR...

December

Sun	Mon	Tue	Wed	Thu	Fri	Sat
1	2	3	4	5	6	7
8	9	10	11	12	13	14
15	16	17	18	19	20	21
22	23	24	25	26	27	28
29	30	31				

_____

_____

_____

_____

_____

_____

I'M THE CEO OF...

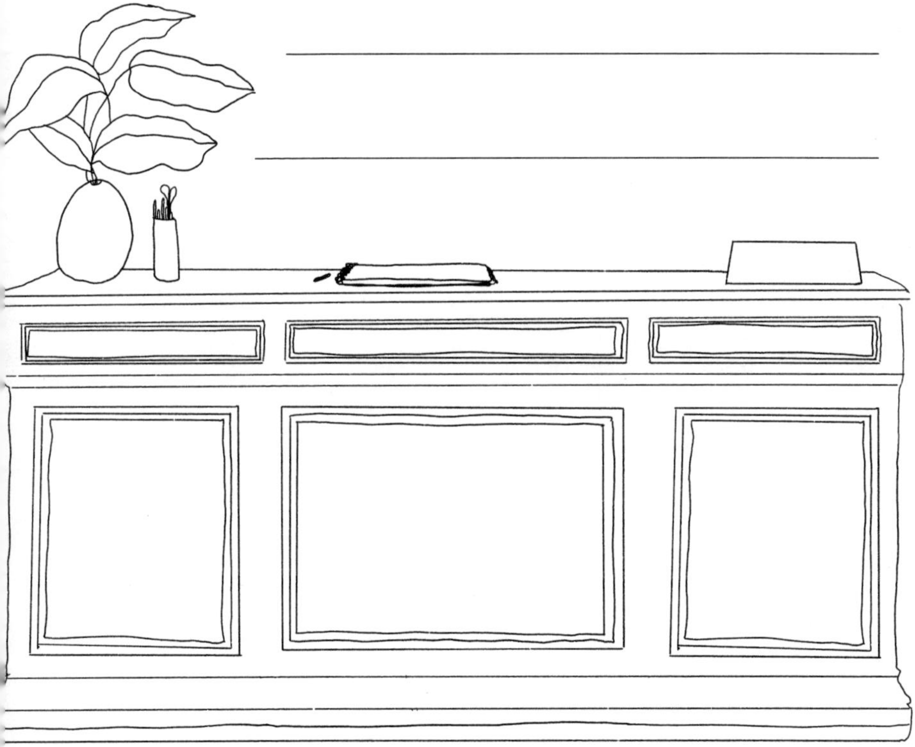

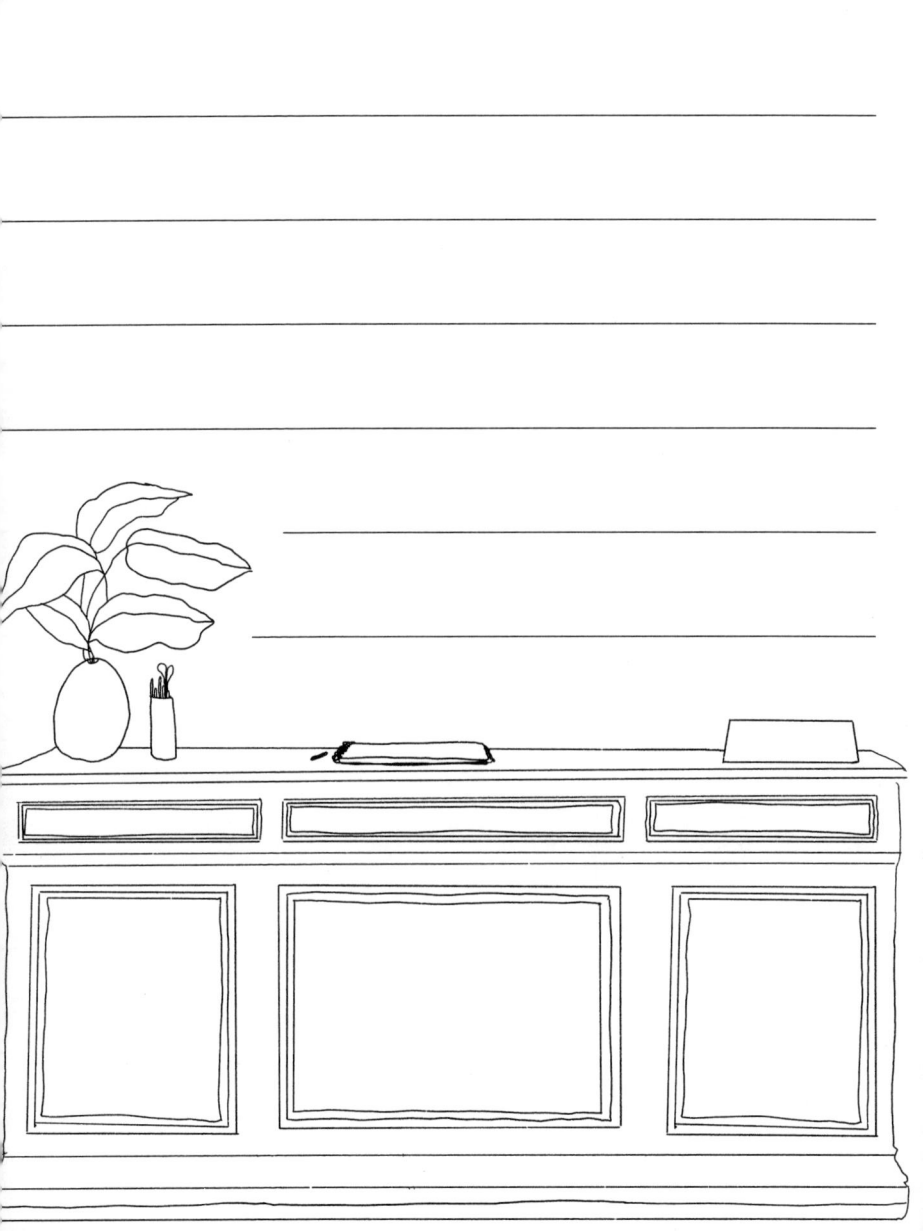

TODAY'S TEA

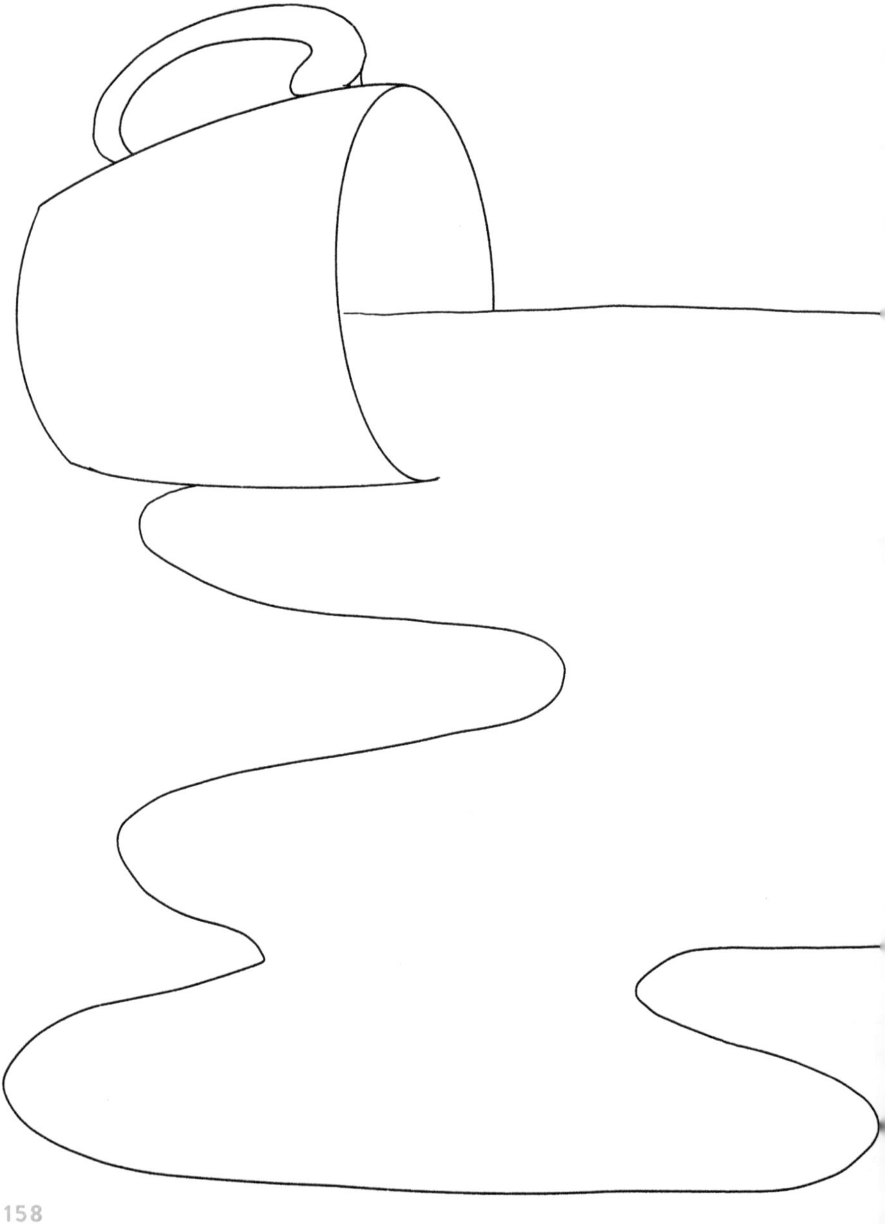

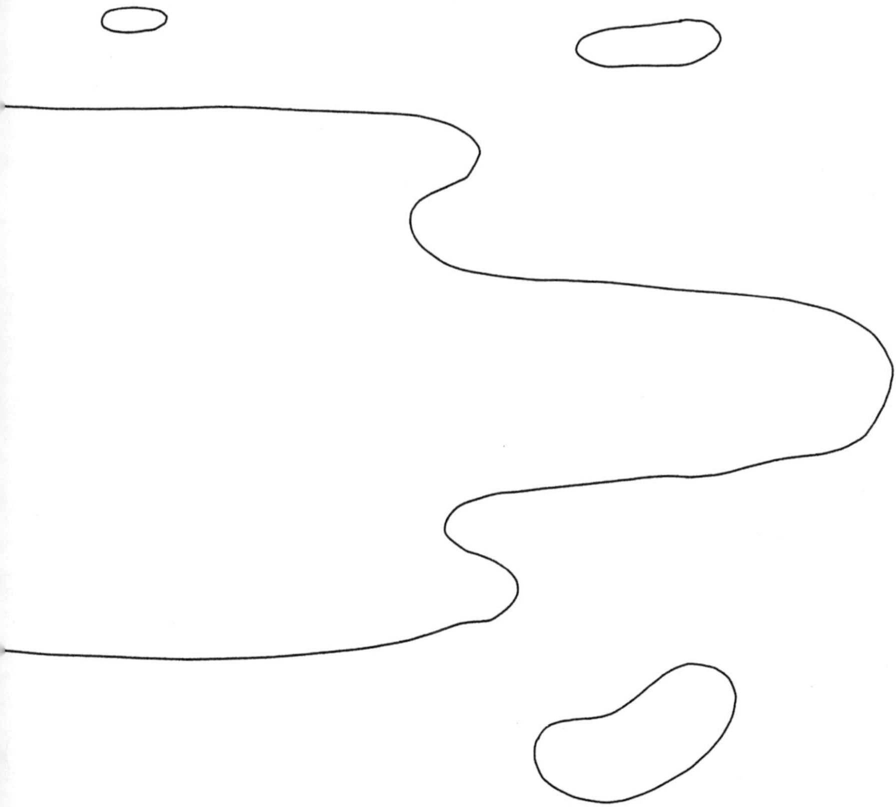

SPOTLIGHT ON...

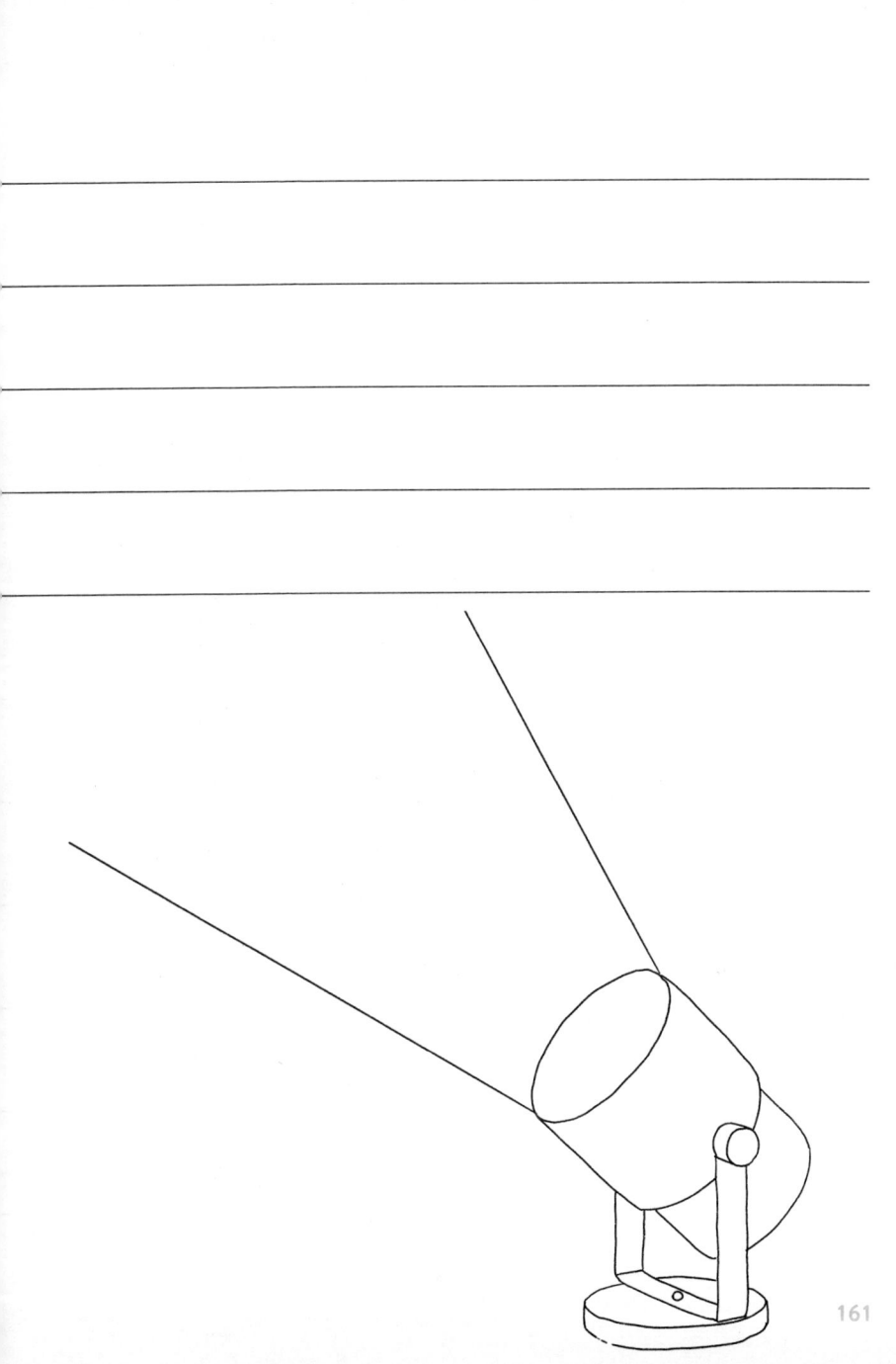

I WONDER...

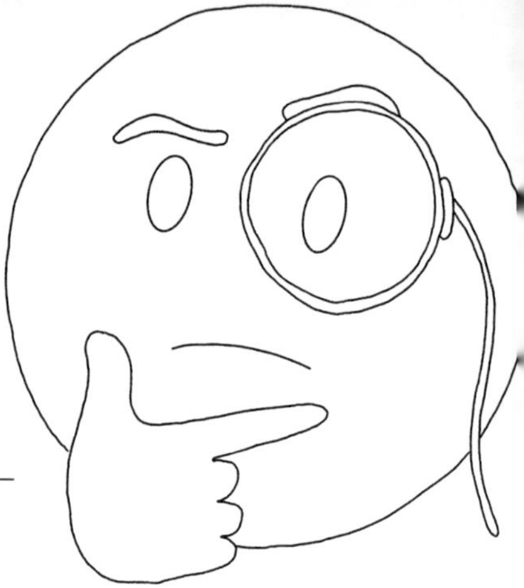

THINGS THAT GO TOGETHER LIKE PB & J

IS THIS NORMAL?

I COULD DO WITHOUT...

NO

THANKS.

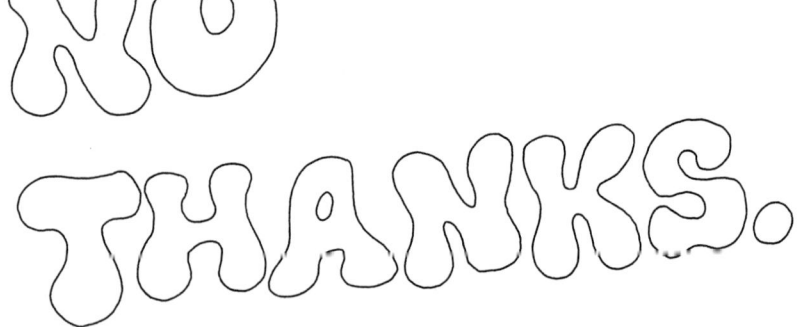

LET'S BRING BACK...

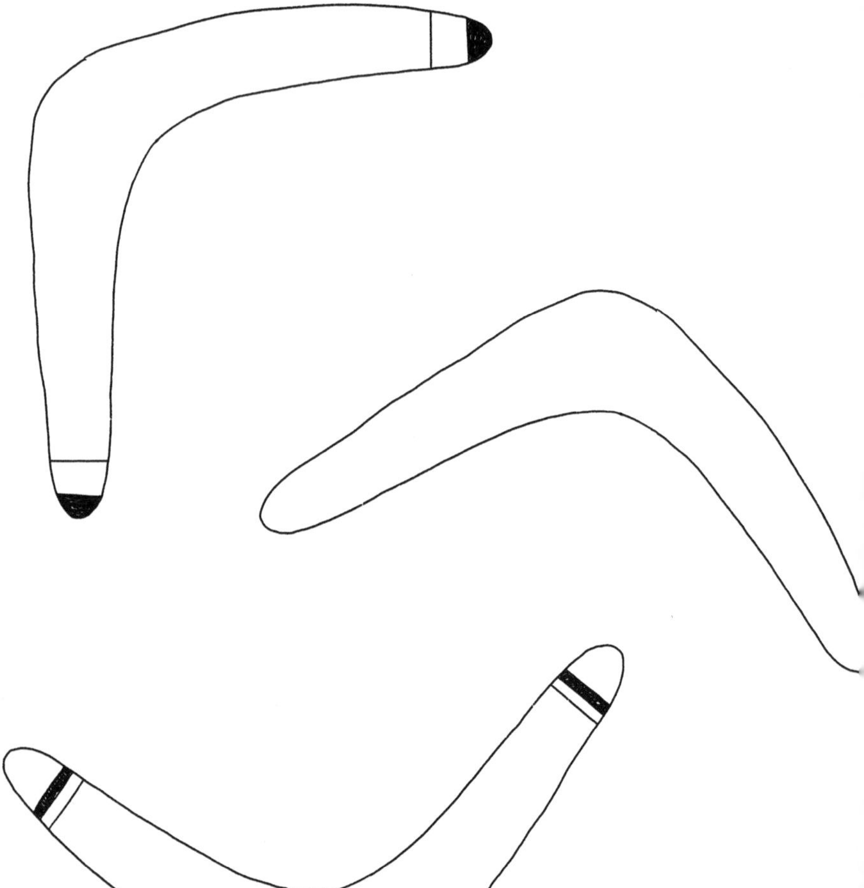

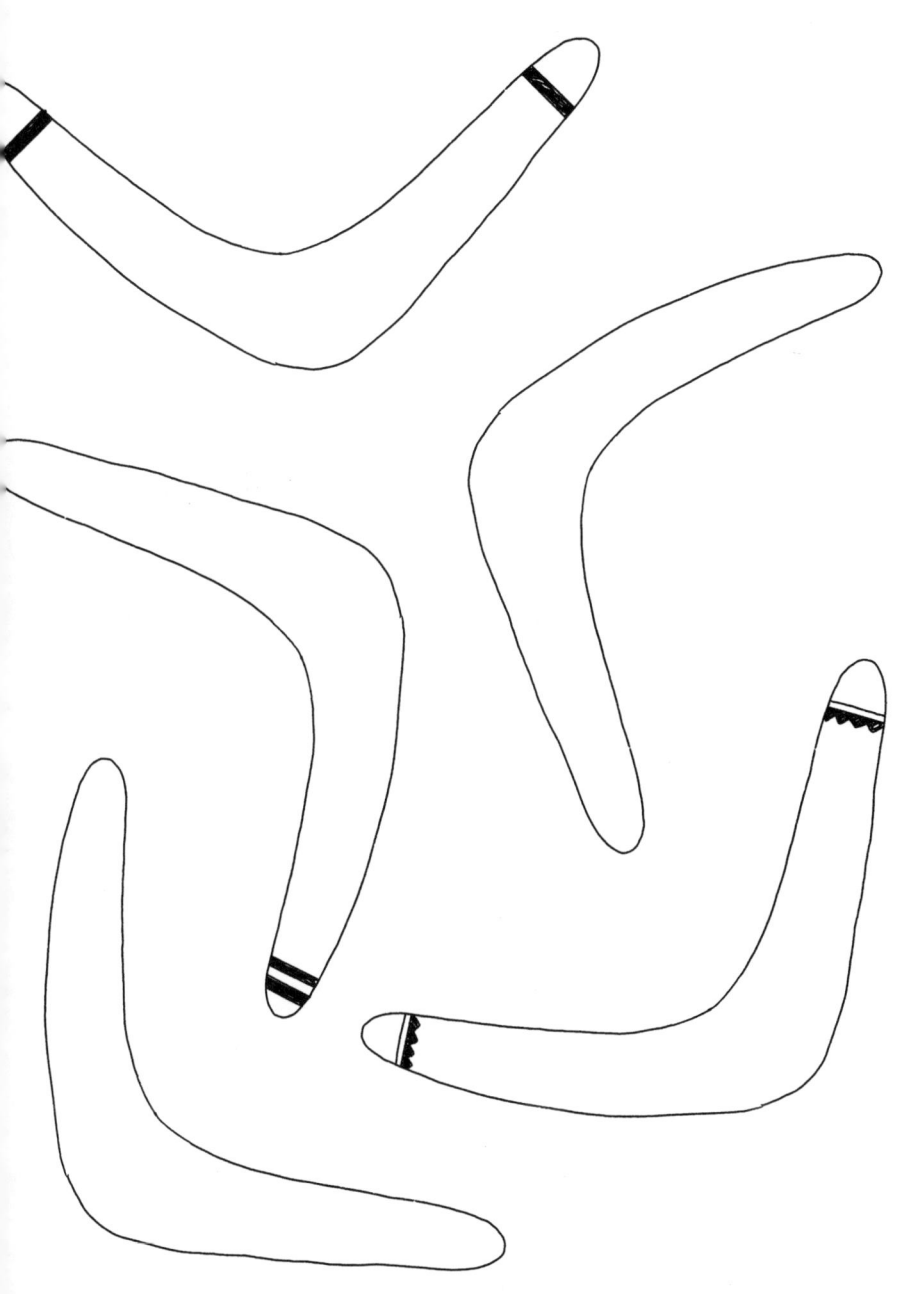

STILL SCROLLING...

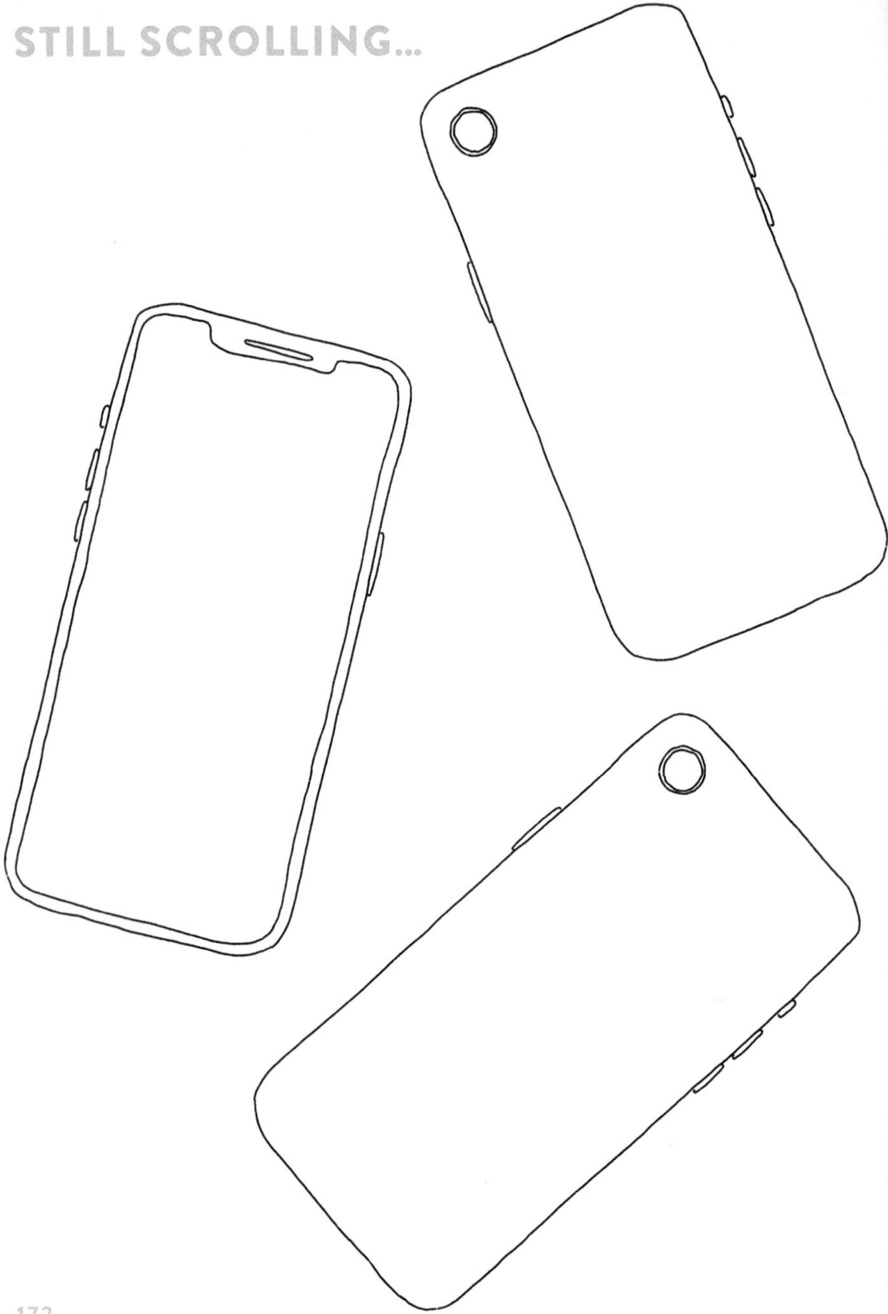

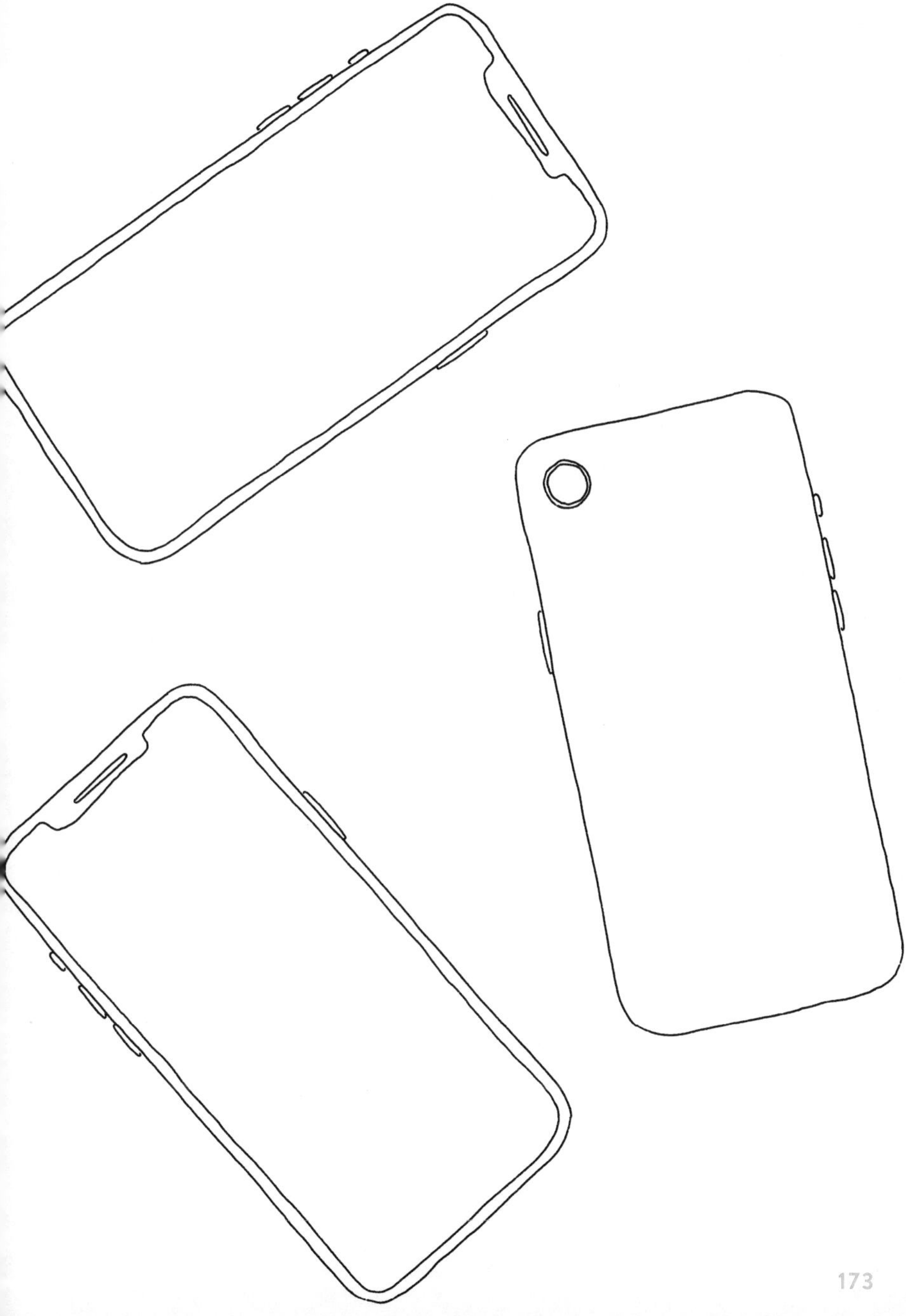

RECEIPTS I'M KEEPING

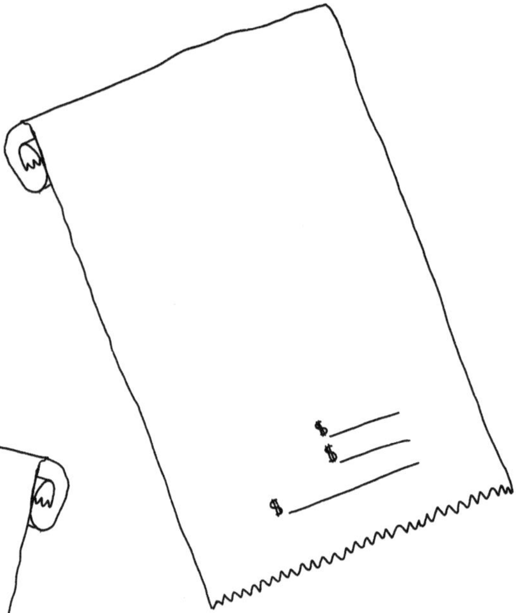
$
$
$

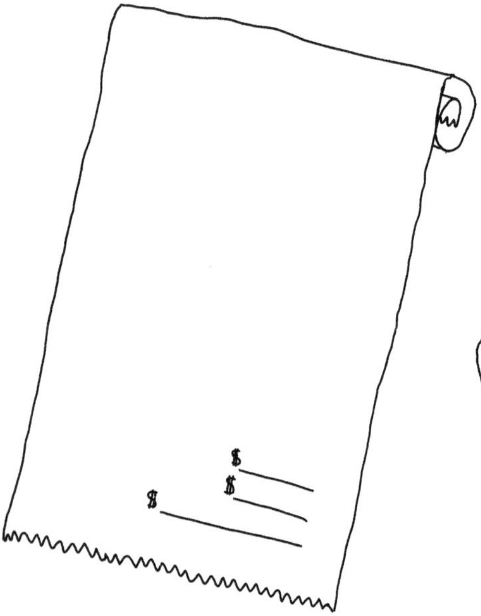
$
$
$

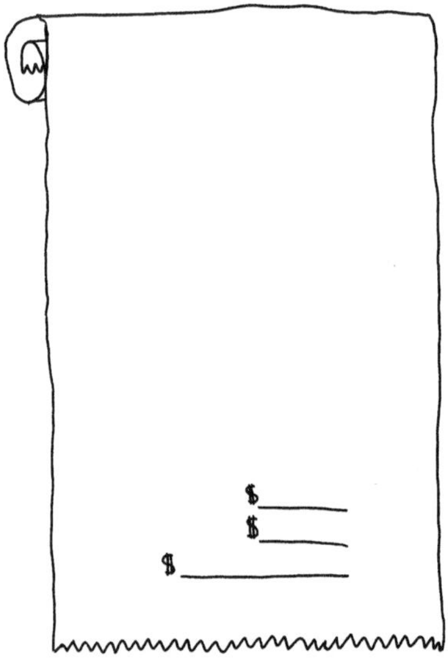
$
$
$

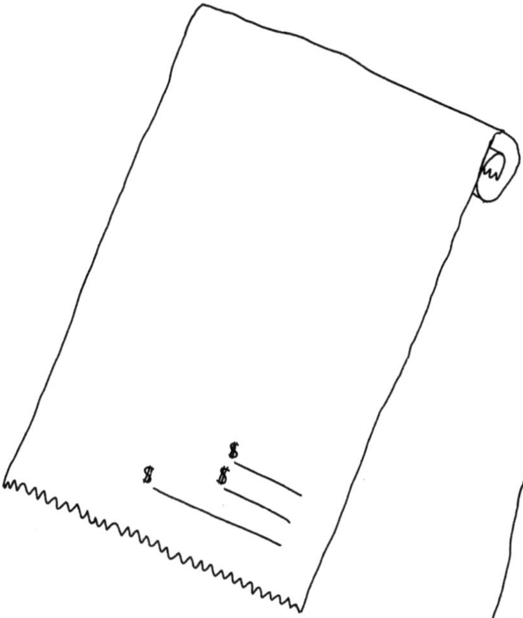

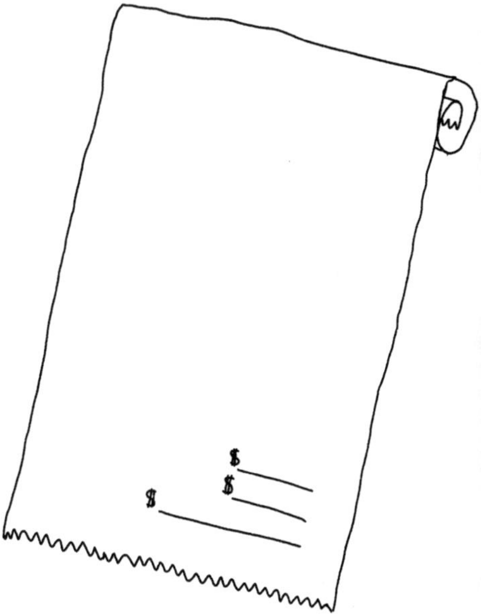

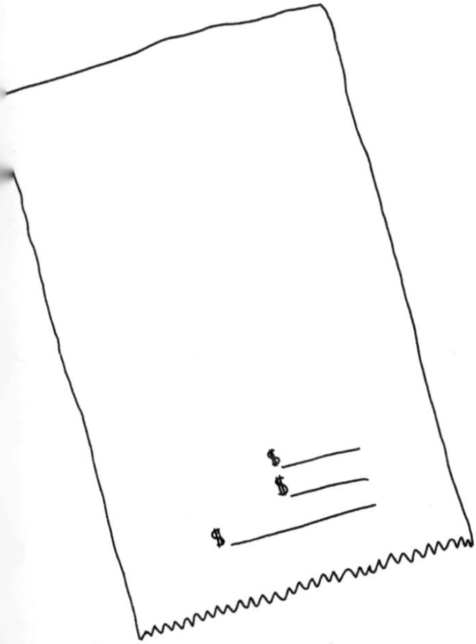

CAN'T WAIT FOR THE NEXT SEASON OF...

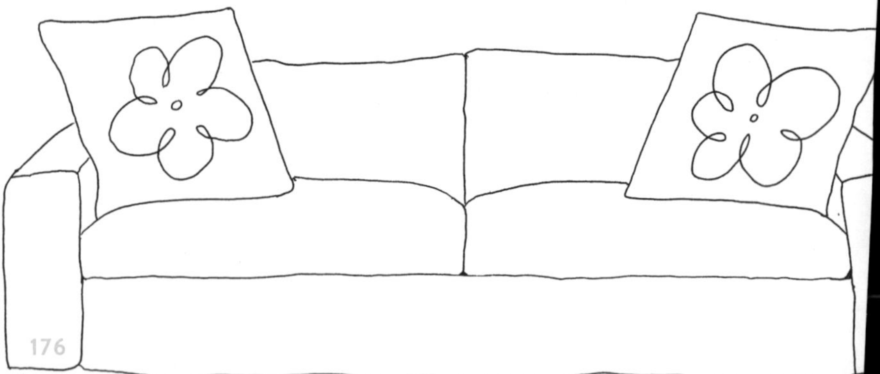